6C $6.00P

THE FROZEN SEA

. . . a book must be the ax for the frozen sea within us.'

THE FROZEN SEA

A Study of Franz Kafka by Charles Neider

New York

RUSSELL & RUSSELL

1962

COPYRIGHT 1948 BY OXFORD UNIVERSITY PRESS, NEW YORK
REISSUED 1962 BY RUSSELL & RUSSELL, INC.
BY ARRANGEMENT WITH THE AUTHOR
L. C. CATALOG CARD NO: 62—16194

PRINTED IN THE UNITED STATES OF AMERICA

For
VIVIEN BRESLOVE NEIDER

TO WHOSE UNDERSTANDING AND GENEROSITY
THIS STUDY LARGELY OWES ITS EXISTENCE

Preface

SOMETIMES, it seems, a work has a will and a way of its own. This book insisted on being born, with a penchant for exegesis surprising to its author. To begin is always difficult, said Tolstoy. Kafka would have replied, To end is torment. I have been as reluctant to end as I was to begin; so many things still want to get said. Yet such is the current Kafka situation that it is advisable to publish the facts herein without further delay.

The discovery of a key to Kafka's novels was made only gradually. My interest in Kafka's dream technique led me to investigate the literature of dream dynamics. I was soon forced to conclude that Kafka had applied Freud's dream findings deliberately. Not only that: he had utilized the core of psychoanalytic knowledge as the basis of his allegorical myths. In addition, he had infused his works with autobiographical details. One recalls Kafka's secretiveness, and his sly remark that there was a secret cabala in his work.

To those readers who are tempted to classify my study as a psychoanalytic one, I should like to say that the presence of psychoanalytic material in my book I consider an accident— Kafka's responsibility, for I am convinced that he deliberately placed it in the novels. By a similar accident I might have stumbled upon a complicated Biblical or mythical or relativity symbolism. The distinction between my approach and the psychoanalytic one is that the latter begins with the psychoanalytic concepts and terminology and ends with a reinforcement and heightening of them; while I begin with nothing but a certain scientific curiosity and tendency to analysis and induction, and end—but only by accident—with a discussion of psychoanalysis. Or to view the distinction a little differently: the psychoanalytic school of literary criticism sees everywhere symbols of the unconscious, without a concern for the artist's conscious desires; in my study I assert above all Kafka's deliberateness or consciousness in his exploitation of such symbols.

A preview of the plan of the book will perhaps be helpful, since the subject matter is complicated and controversial. I begin with an extended analysis of the Kafka literature, with emphasis on its shortcomings and their effect on Kafka's vogue. Chapter II presents in broad terms a new aspect of Kafka which, after the biographical chapter, Chapter III, is studied in detail for the next two chapters. Up to this point the treatment does not presuppose a special key, but in Chapters VI and VII the secret key is discussed. In order to avoid confusion and unnecessary complication, the discussion of the key and its implications is delayed until more traditional ground has been covered. For reasons of space and also because of my disinclination to clutter this study with citations of authority, I assume on the reader's part, during these two chapters, an intimate knowledge of psychoanalytic literature. The reader is warned that none of the intellectual constructs and symbol-constructions are my own. I am indebted for them to the Freudian psychology, and am responsible only for their elucidation in Kafka's works.

The question poses itself: Are there clues to Kafka's secret in his diaries? The fragmentary diaries now available are almost totally silent on this point. Most of the diaries and the greater part of the important *Letter to My Father* have never been published. These are in the custody of Max Brod, who has promised to release them in the near future. The answer waits upon their publication.

An interesting study, outside the scope of this book, could be written on Kafka and the failure of nerve in our century, indicating Kafka's relation to the religious faction of the German expressionist movement, which includes such figures as Barlach, Werfel, Edschmid, and Kornfeld. It would be interesting to view Kafka, also, from the perspective of such contemporary revivalists as Auden, Eliot, Huxley, *et al.*, and to examine his influence on them as well as the influence of the German religious revival upon supernaturalists in England and America. An investigation of Kafka's influence upon naturalists (mainly in terms of technique and psychology) as well as upon supernaturalists would also be illuminating. Finally, a detailed examination of the influence of the religious revival in relation to criticism and interpretation of Kafka would be valuable. But at present it is appropriate to indicate only that the expressionist movement was not solely religious (it included rational expressionists who desired social and political reforms), that it arose from a dissatisfaction with a stagnant, spiritless society as well as with current modes in art and literature, and that Kafka avoided identifying himself—at least in his work—with any of the three or four factions of the movement.

CHARLES NEIDER

Christmas, 1947

Acknowledgments

QUOTATIONS from Franz Kafka's *Amerika* are from the translation by Edwin Muir, copyright 1946, by New Directions, and are reprinted by permission of New Directions; those from *The Trial* and *The Castle* are from the translations by Willa and Edwin Muir, copyright 1937, and 1930, 1941, respectively, by Alfred A. Knopf, Inc., and are reprinted by permission of Alfred A. Knopf, Inc.; those from *The Great Wall of China* are from the translation by Willa and Edwin Muir, copyright 1946, by Schocken Books, New York, and are reprinted by permission of Schocken Books; those from *Franz Kafka: A Biography,* by Max Brod, are from the translations by G. Humphreys Roberts and by Sophie Prombaum, copyright 1947, by Schocken Books, New York, and 1946, by Twice A Year Press, respectively, and are reprinted by permission of Schocken Books and Twice A Year Press. The quotation from Kafka's 'Meditations' is from *A Franz Kafka Miscellany,* copyright 1946, by Twice A Year Press, and is reprinted by permission of Twice A Year Press.

It is a pleasure to thank Klaus Mann, Frederic Morton, F. C. Weiskopf, and René Wellek for their comments on the manuscript, and Dr. Frederic Wertham for his comments on the proofs. I wish to thank R. H. P. Senhouse of Martin Secker and Warburg, Ltd., for his kind personal co-operation. I wish especially to thank Mark Neider for his invaluable reading of the proofs.

Contents

Franz Kafka and the Cabalists

ONLY a little more than twenty years ago there died in Europe a comparatively young man who wrote some of the most extraordinary books of modern times, books of great daring, brilliance, and profundity. Although these books have been known and appreciated by only a few, they offer a rich experience to the many.

Take *The Castle*—a novel full of wonder and suspense, strange happenings, and a moody and poetic atmosphere suggestive of a heath, a novel that sets up waves in the reader which affect him long after he has put it down; a novel of a man who dies of exhaustion from seeking logic and justice on earth. Or take *The Trial*—a great, novel-length detective story in which the hero feels his life is threatened, in which he is pursued by an enemy whose nature is unclear to him but who stalks him unfalteringly and with 'insidious intent' until he is slain; a novel full of strange houses, and dim, dangerous apartments, and queer and dangerous people.

Beautifully wrought and deceptively simple, the profundity of these novels is unobtrusive. The novels please by their remarkable form and their sensory stimulation. Their symbolism is complex but its effect is emotional and psychological and does not depend on intellectual efforts.

Kafka is an expert at contriving a complicated and effective plot and at generating an immense amount of suspense. He is not a conventionally realistic novelist who sprinkles his canvas with samples of humanity, in the manner of Balzac and Tolstoy; nor is he, like James Joyce, a fine etcher of a few thoroughly realized individuals, although some of his characters possess outstanding individual traits. Kafka is not interested in delineating characters as such; his interest lies rather in the most profound and highly personal psychological factors. Yet his people are anything but drab and mechanical. They are as startling as Dostoyevsky's—probably because of Kafka's unflagging and uncanny interest in the hidden causes of certain types of abnormal behavior.

Kafka writes about Everyman. He writes about him almost in the medieval allegorical sense and adds pungent irony and stunning psychological insight. But his characters are also symbols in the modern tradition: that is, they are symbolic on several levels at the same time. In fact, the entire texture of his novels is shot through with symbolism. Yet, strangely enough, this does not overburden them or make them opaque or ineffective. On the contrary, under Kafka's hand it lends them an evocative and allusive quality rarely duplicated in modern literature, and this quality heightens the enjoyment of the reader as well as his sense of perceiving the truth.

What of Kafka's style? It is brilliant and simple; it is classical. Perhaps Kafka's sole prose eccentricity is his occasional use of long paragraphs, in which dialogue may be presented without indentation. His settings are bizarre, not intrinsically but because of his poetic gift of selecting and heightening those elements in a normal environment which he wishes to employ for a fantastic effect. *The Trial,* for example, is laid in a city, *The Castle,* in a village; and the interesting thing is that these are at once both real and dreamlike environments. To a large extent Kafka's genius lies in this ability to fluctuate precariously between the solid and the insubstantial, between realism and distortion. The emotional effect on the reader of this talent of Kafka's is overpowering.

Kafka's father was a highly successful businessman, a 'regular' fellow, whom Kafka, in his youth, despaired of emulating because of his physical fragility as compared with his father's robustness, and because of his leaning toward the artistic. Kafka never got on with his father; his father was puzzled by him and antagonistic, while Kafka himself was full of guilt and resentment, reactions he never outgrew. Kafka was a Jew. He was also a civil servant, very familiar with the bureaucracy of the semifeudalistic Austrian Empire. And, finally, he was sickly—he died of tuberculosis in 1924. All of these elements are germane to an understanding of his work and of the fact that Kafka's protagonists are ridden by fears and guilt and that they strive compulsively toward equilibrium until exhausting themselves to death. His heroes live in a nightmare of reality, a reality responding to the laws, to the distortions of the dream world.

In view of all this, it is ironic that Kafka, who of all modern writers perhaps most bitterly satirized cabalism, should himself be the victim, after his death, of a number of cabalas whose proponents are increasing and, if anything, growing even more ardent and esoteric. The cabalists are not limited to country or school; their abundant literature flourishes; and only occasionally does one hear a voice in protest. Kafka has come close to becoming the exclusive literary property of esoteric readers; the fact is, regardless whether he would have approved of it or not, he is not getting through to his maximum audience.

Of the several cabalas the most prominent are the mystic and the psychoanalytic. Even the Marxist method, which prides itself on its skeptical and earth-bound approach, at times threatens to expand to the nebulousness of a cabala, with strange and startling effects. Much of the cabalism can be set down as the result of critical professionalism: over-complication and temporary blindness are the specialist's occupational hazards. There has been a critical tendency in the past few decades to write around a subject and to avoid a direct examination and discussion of works themselves, as though the latter were too simple a task to occupy a really worth-while critical intelligence. However, in a world beset by chaos and lack of faith the search for meaning, for a 'key,' is particularly intense. Since Kafka is a refreshing voice, he has been seized upon by critics bored with an overplayed realism; and since his manner is extremely allusive it is natural that the interpretations of his work and life should be so varied, passionate, and so often mistaken.

The misinterpretation of Kafka is threefold: literary, critical, and philosophical. In the first place various conclusions have been formed regarding the structure, style, and psychology of Kafka's works that are not warranted by the facts, such as the supposed relation between Joseph K. of *The Trial* and K. of *The Castle,* and the thematic and psychological differences between these two novels. In the second place, critics have read into Kafka meanings unsupported by sufficient internal proof, and in a number of cases have made interesting but unfounded comments based on poor reasoning and/or on false stress and anachronisms. In the third place the philosophical issues in the Kafka quarrel have been obscured by most of the commentators. The Kafka problem should be viewed in the light of the world-wide religious revival which has been accelerating during the past several decades and which is, deplorably, to a large extent responsible for the mystical interpretations of Kafka as exemplified by Brod and other of Kafka's mystical friends, by his excellent and articulate mystical English translator, Edwin Muir, and by those converts to antinaturalism or supernaturalism who have

[6]

looked upon Kafka possessively as well as admiringly—Auden, Isherwood, Huxley, and the rest. The Kafka problem is not isolated from literary matters. The philosophical and therefore the ethical and political implications of the religious revival, of the 'failure of nerve,' are deep and ramified, as John Dewey, Sidney Hook, Morris R. Cohen, and other naturalists have made clear. The revivalists have beaten the drum loudest for Kafka; they have sought far and earnestly for aids to their movement. In the case of Kafka, however, they have trundled a Trojan horse into their camp.

The entire Kafka controversy has been incredibly muddled, with both sides wandering into enemy territory and sniping at their own positions. In the main the supernaturalists have come out best under such conditions, not because of superior logic but because, based on the vague and the unempirical, they have fought the battle on their own ground. They have, in a sense, laid down the rules of the game, with their 'inside' knowledge as divulged by Kafka's intimates and disciples, their exegeses in terms of absolutes, the divine, and original sin.

The naturalist critics, deceived by the belief that the controversy is only literary after all, have failed to recognize the philosophical issues and the moral consequences implicit in the Kafka problem. Perhaps they are fascinated by the fantastic logic of the mystics, or perhaps they have succumbed to the lure of the 'key.' In any event, they appear to have accepted as gospel reports from the disciples, even when these are clearly at variance with their own reasoning and with the evidence in the works of Kafka. In certain cases the naturalists have even adopted some of the impedimenta of the supernaturalists. Their position might be: (1) If Kafka is found, on the basis of the best evidence, internal and external, to be supernatural, then he should be read simply for whatever artistic values he possesses apart from his ideas, presupposing

[7]

that a divorce between these is possible. His life and work should then be studied for the light it casts upon the failure of nerve in our century. (2) If, because of insufficient evidence, no conclusion can be formed concerning Kafka's philosophical position, it should be made clear that he is not the special province of the mystics, and he should then be read by the naturalists for ethical as well as aesthetic reasons. But witness their silence, their uncertainty, and their occasional gullibility. At best they deny the assertion of the mystics that Kafka is *solely* concerned with the incommensurability between man and God, and they proceed to suggest other relevant and illuminating matter. Sometimes they ignore the business of the divine out of embarrassment; but generally they accept the premise and then struggle to get a firm grip on Kafka despite it. The supernaturalists, of course, abhor empirical method as a means of warranting assertions and they are consistent in neglecting it in their discussions of Kafka. It is all the more curious, then, that the naturalists have neglected the factors of observation, analysis, supposition, idealization, and inference in their attempts to confute them.

Both the naturalist and the anti- or supernaturalist interpretations of Kafka are legitimate, the first on the basis of the absence of explicit references to supernatural beliefs and motifs in Kafka and the second on the basis of biographical data relating to Kafka's preoccupation with mystical doctrine. The naturalist approach significantly places first emphasis on Kafka's strange relations with his father, while the supernaturalist more or less neglects these in favor of disembodied ideas, impulses, and beliefs. The naturalist approach may even grant the existence of the supernaturalist element in Kafka's work, and then interpret it as a projection of his personal situation, in the light of its knowledge of the inception and development of religious myths. But it need not go so far, for the burden of proof lies with the supernaturalists,

[8]

since it is they who insist on meanings in Kafka which are not self-evident.

It does not follow that a man necessarily writes about his beliefs, particularly where the novel form is concerned, whether he wishes to do so or not. It remains, therefore, for the mystics to prove that the works contain unified and fertile ramifications on the religious theme. To date they have failed to do this; they are always pointing out the emperor's finery when it is obvious he is naked, they are forever asking the reader to assume the existence of allegories which are not in the books but which they require to complete their text.

The naturalist's position is much simpler and easier; his interpretation neglects no element of the Kafka problem. He deals with details as parts of a whole and rather than ask the reader to assume the existence of the nonexistent, he offers him new light on both the man and his work by the careful examination of facts related to the whole. As for the question why Kafka did not make his religious notions explicit in his work, here again the burden of proof rests upon the mystics. The naturalist can content himself with the assumption that Kafka had sufficient (and perhaps anti-religious) reasons for remaining vague regarding his mysticism; at any rate he can peacefully accept the fact that the answer is unknown and proceed to an examination of the known facts with a view to reaching a conclusion. Another aspect of the case favoring the naturalist is that even if Kafka did write about the divine, it does not follow that his books do not possess a secular, more fruitful meaning. One may believe one is writing about God yet actually write about men; and this is a fair probability in any case, since one can write only in terms of one's mortal experience. The naturalist, then, can reach the conclusion that what Kafka is writing about is not the incommensurability between man and the divine, but between Kafka and his father or Kafka and society, and that basically he is asserting

[9]

that to reach a spiritual understanding with his father and/or society is as impossible as reaching the castle or the highest court.

It must not be forgotten that a book is a public property and that it may, and quite often does, have an effect altogether different from the author's intention. For this added reason it is important to insist on Kafka's books speaking for themselves —that is, to insist on an internal examination of them for casting light on his meaning. At the present time each major book of his published in English contains material written either by Brod or by Muir, not to mention others, prejudicing the innocent reader in favor of the mystical point of view. Thus a sort of, perhaps involuntary, proselytizing is carried on. If Kafka's books need prefaces and epilogues, then it is time that the naturalist had an opportunity to present his views side by side with the mystic, in order that the reader may come to his own conclusions after examining all the evidence.

The chief advocates of the mystical school—by far the greatest cabala of them all—are Max Brod and Edwin Muir.

Appreciators of the work of Franz Kafka owe an incalculable debt to Max Brod, his friend, literary executor, and biographer. Convinced that Kafka was a genius, Brod exerted himself on Kafka's behalf during the latter's lifetime. After his death, by refusing to abide by his friend's posthumous request that his manuscripts be destroyed, he preserved the three novels and much of the shorter fiction and diaries, as well as the *Letter to My Father*. A good deal of what is known about Kafka is to be found in Brod's biography, which was first published in Prague in 1937, the year the final volume of the *Gesammelte Schriften* appeared. In 1945-6 it was published in France and England. The history of its publication parallels the history of the Kafka revival.

In a curious sense Kafka is Max Brod's creation. Brod

is largely if not altogether responsible for the theological interpretation. It was he who first characterized Kafka's theme as the incommensurability between man and the divine, and who spoke of man's attempt to achieve divine justice in *The Trial* and divine grace in *The Castle*. Brod, the ardent Zionist, has even written of Kafka's works as if they were secret Zionist tracts. To one who finds the theological interpretations totally unsupported by internal evidence, and who believes that they have misrepresented Kafka's meaning, Brod's critical influence appears unfortunate.

Early in his biography Brod introduces extensive excerpts from Kafka's *Letter to My Father* in order to illuminate Kafka's childhood. He values the *Letter* highly, yet accepts only those portions which suit his bias. He is biased not only against psychoanalysis but against scientific method as a whole. His attitude toward psychoanalysis is explicit, his attitude toward science implicit in his emphasis on 'deeper realities,' 'higher realities,' absolutes, and references to the 'inferior' truths of science. The fact is that Kafka was secretive. One wonders whether Brod possesses sufficient information regarding Kafka's personal life, obtained from sources other than Kafka, to warrant making judgments contrary to Kafka's own, as expressed in the *Letter*. Brod's bias prevents him from understanding the therapeutic nature of much art. To sickly artists like Kafka, art is at least as much, if not more, a means to an end than the end itself. Brod deduces from this that the emphasis on means is an emphasis on religion.

Because of the looseness of his terminology, it is not always easy to understand Brod's meaning. At times he uses the word 'religious' in a metaphysical sense and at others he means it to be synonymous with heightened living or poetic idealism. He is fond of writing in terms of unconditionals and finalities, terms that, especially when referring to human beings, are not to be applied lightly. What Brod means by the

[11]

father's 'nature' or anyone's 'nature' is unclear, but it is obvious that 'nature' and 'character' are conceived by him as unchangeable as Platonic absolutes. The word 'absolute' occurs frequently in the biography. 'A characteristic that places him in the category of a saint was his absolute faith,' he writes. Yet elsewhere he speaks of Kafka's profound skepticism.

Brod firmly believes that Kafka's tragedy was essentially caused 'by the fact that a man so tremendously richly gifted, with such a rich creative urge, was forced just at the time when his youthful strength was unfolding itself, to work day in day out to the point of exhaustion, doing things which inwardly didn't interest him in the least.' He does not believe that the roots of the tragedy lay in Kafka's relations with his father, i.e. his neurosis, although he admits that 'only in so far as his exaggerated feeling of his tie with his father held him firm in the bonds of his profession did it contribute to the disaster. . .' He sees Kafka's illness as the result of a heroic conflict between a rich creative urge and an inimical external environment, deprecating the importance of a father tie even while admitting that the tie may have prevented Kafka from withdrawing from the environment.

Brod fails to understand the masochistic implications of a severe neurosis. Curiously enough, since he cannot, in his own terms, explain Kafka's inability to leave the environment of his profession, he leans upon Kafka's neurosis to explain this inability while denying the importance of neurosis in Kafka. He does not explain why Kafka succumbed to the job although less fortunate writers and artists have created and lived successfully under worse conditions. Nor does he indicate how his thesis would explain Kafka's inability to marry F.B.

Brod is weakest in the chapter on religious development. Those who hope to obtain documentation on Kafka's religious interests will be disappointed. They will find nothing concretely theological. They will find such statements as 'Kafka

[12]

disputes with God as Job once did. He disputes about original sin, and Paradise Lost.' They will find theological interpretations of neurotic phenomena. And these will often be highly sectarian. For example: ' "To be near God" and "to live rightly" were identical for Kafka. As a member of a race without a country one cannot live properly. This almost realistically Jewish interpretation of Kafka, in which Zionism is a way of life of almost religious relevance, I shall endeavour to develop later on.'

Significantly, Brod obliquely admits that Kafka was not explicit about the question of religion. 'For all his mourning over the imperfection and intransparency of human actions, Kafka was convinced that there were truths which could not be assailed. He did not express this in words, but he did so by his whole behaviour all his life.' Yet he presumes to reveal Kafka's explicit meaning in theological terms. 'The Absolute is there—but it is incommensurable with the life of man—this would seem to be a fundamental experience of Kafka's'; 'The eternal misunderstanding between God and man induces Kafka . . .'; 'the failure of man in the sight of God'; 'For this reason the divine world becomes for us a transcendental territory, and in the truest sense of the words, strange, uncanny. To our ears the will of God sounds illogical, that is to say opposed to our human logic in a grotesque fashion. . .'

Brod quotes from Job as if it were the court of final appeal. He becomes involved in a sort of heavenly geometry. He flagellates facts. In short, he indulges in the very human process of expressing himself; it is Brod he reveals, not Kafka. He no more succeeds in revealing Kafka than he does in revealing God.

Muir carries Brod's suggestion to an extreme. To him the novels are definitely metaphysical or theological; he accepts the word 'divine' literally, compares the novels to various religious works, among them *Pilgrim's Progress*, and sees

[13]

Kafka's creations as elaborate religious allegories of a highly personal nature. Brod, however, does not go so far. He makes it clear that a biographical understanding of the novels is more vital than theological explanations. But Muir, apparently unsatisfied with this rather pragmatic view of the divine, constructs case after case to implement his contention that Kafka's works follow the lines of mystical revelation. His skilfully contrived cases recall the hair-splitting of the schoolmen.

An essay by Albert Camus, entitled 'Hope and Absurdity,' reveals some striking insights into the nature of the absurd in Kafka, into some of Kafka's more subtle mannerisms and into his tragic effects. But essentially the essay is weak and in the end adds little to a real understanding of Kafka. The reason for this is Camus's adherence to the theological conceptions of Kafka, his dependence on the usual mystical categories and on the usual comparisons with Kierkegaard. Camus is at his best when speaking of aesthetic matters; when he enters the realm of meaning and interpretation he spreads darkness around him like a shroud. He is sensible until he begins to speak of God and the supernatural, wholly accepting these major premises without offering definitions or proof. Camus's essay is largely rhetorical. Like all the perorations of the mystagogues, it is an improvisation on unsustained premises. His approach is not genetic. It is a method *in vacuo*. It restates the old mystical line, this time in the existentialist framework. His essay contains such sentences as these: 'The fatal error of giving to God what is not God's is also the subject of this episode of *The Castle*. But for Kafka, it seems that this is not an error. It is a doctrine and a "leap." There is nothing which is not God's.' Again: 'Amalia, the eldest sister, has rejected the shameful proposition made her by one of the functionaries of the castle. The immoral curse which followed this has forever rejected her from the love of God. To be incapable of sacrificing one's honor for God is to become

[14]

unworthy of His grace.' Camus, needless to say, makes no effort to indicate how he concluded that Sortini represents God, much less how he knows that God exists.

A shrewd American exegete of the mystical school is John Kelly. By the use of hindsight and a careful selection of odd bits from *The Trial,* he builds up a case to show that Kafka was deliberately theological and neo-Calvinist, and that at the same time, immersed in Kierkegaard, he was also expressing without knowing it a parallel to *Commentary on the Epistle to the Romans,* by Kierkegaard's disciple Karl Barth. His constant implication is that Kafka's effects and suggestions are cerebral and purposive to an almost political degree. Kelly does not discuss Kafka in biographical or social terms, or in literary or psychoanalytical ones. To Kelly, Kafka is an automaton intent on the game of translating Kierkegaard into novelistic equivalents.

Not all the mystical apologists, however, are as shrewd and as closely reasoned as Kelly. An English writer, R. H. Thomas, in his essay entitled 'Franz Kafka and the Religious Aspect of Expressionism,' maintains that the subject of Kafka's work is the attempt 'to reconcile the Finite with the Infinite.' In the same breath in which he talks of the infinite in terms of the finite, however, Thomas calls *The Metamorphosis* 'a significant document of the war period,' claiming that 'the sudden change in Samsa is to be regarded as the symbolical presentation of the dissolution of the prevailing order of things, such as took place under the impact of the war.' Even the most historically minded and sociological of the Kafka critics have hesitated to go this far. Coming from one who accepts enthusiastically Brod's dictum of divine grace and justice, it points up with startling clarity just how confused is so much of the thinking on Kafka.

Nor is Thomas free of bald factual errors. For example: 'In 1923 he went to Berlin where he suffered from malnutrition at the time of the deepest economic distress in Germany. He married [*sic!*] in the same year but he was already a hopeless invalid.' Thomas makes another error, which caused some anguished soul to write 'No!' in the margin of a library copy of the essay: he calls *Amerika* the last of Kafka's novels—that is, he does so for one sentence. In the next sentence he corrects himself chronologically, only to pile confusion on confusion by adding: 'Although chronologically it precedes the other two (it was begun in 1912) it must be regarded, by virtue of its content, as following upon them.' Why does he make the statement? The answer is (begging pardon for a *non sequitur*): 'For in this work Kafka suggests the possibility of a happy ending of fulfilment and thus it stands apart from most of his work.'

I mention Mr. Thomas's factual errors only in order to indicate the state of Kafka literature. Here are two others from *Transition Stories,* edited by Eugene Jolas and Robert Sage: 'Franz Kafka was born in Czechoslovakia and died in Germany in 1924 at the age of thirty years.' 'He published nothing during his lifetime.' And both Hannah Arendt and Janko Lavrin keep speaking of *Amerika* as Kafka's last novel, probably because when it first appeared in 1927 it followed *Der Prozess* (1925) and *Das Schloss* (1926) and because these writers may have referred to those editions. Frederick J. Hoffman says that Kafka 'was the only one of three sons who had survived birth.' According to Clement Greenberg, Kafka was 'the only son among four children. . .' Both are in error. Kafka had two brothers and three sisters; the two brothers died, one at two, the other at a year and a half. Greenberg calls *The Trial* the only complete novel of Kafka. Apparently he has overlooked the fragments published in the *Gesammelte Schriften.*

Whereas Kelly utilizes reason in an attempt to prove mysticism in Kafka, Ezequiel Martínez Estrada, in his 'The

[16]

Contours of Kafka's World,' uses mysticism itself in a similar attempt. 'The most direct route to an interpretation of Kafka is not that which leads straight to conclusions,' says Estrada. He then proceeds to an orgy of wildest postulation, mainly about 'pure' reason and 'pure' intuition. He is full of historical oddities—e.g. he speaks of poets, philosophers, and scientists at the beginning of this century as 'weakening or denying the heretofore unquestioned rights of the postulates of reason and the certitudes of common sense.' This disregards the contribution of Schopenhauer, among others, relating to the significance of the unconscious. Estrada asserts the 'absolute, mathematical security' of the new, modern world, which is the sort of thing said loudly in every boastful age, often to be exploded by the next major discovery. He calls intuition the 'new technique for understanding and divining the nature of the world,' as if the great artists and the saints and mystics of past centuries were not historical facts. Kafka, he asserts, 'applies the new tool of pure intuition to the observation and chronicling of the reality of man in an alien world.' This artificial dichotomy between 'pure' reason and 'pure' intuition has no valid connection with reality. The character of the 'new' world of relativity and the universe of neo-vitalism can be divined only by intuition, says Estrada. But who operates in the higher mathematical realms of relativity—in, say, perceiving the fourth dimension—by intuition alone? Where would Einstein have got in his physical research early in the century without the empiricism of the Michelson-Morley experiments and their failure to register 'ether' drag? How could he have conceived of his relativity theory before being aware of the problem? And who achieves a solely intuitive grasp of a world of n dimensions, which only mathematics offers in pragmatic form? One of the lessons to be learned from Einstein is that we must never cease being skeptical of our 'intuition,' which is largely dependent on sense impressions and which therefore is more valid in terrestrial

[17]

terms than in universal ones—in terms, say, of velocities far
beyond human experience or 'colors' beyond the range of
human vision. On the other hand we must also be skeptical
of 'reason.'

There seems to be no limit to the confusion of much of
Kafka literature. And some of it is remarkably vulgar. Denis
Saurat, for example, calls *The Castle* 'a perfect triumph of
German art.' He continues: 'For a German who is perfectly
understood is a German deflated: his ultimate meaning is
commonplace, trivial, or puerile. . . Therefore a true artist,
if he be a German, draws a veil over his meaning and casts
his spell on you by his manner; your journey leads nowhere,
but you have the great pleasure of the journey.' Saurat asserts
that to have left *The Castle* unfinished was a marvelous stroke
on the part of Kafka, because 'we are left on the brink of an
abyss, and full of wonderment.' To leave a work unfinished
is the height of German art, thinks Saurat. 'It would have been
better for *Faust*, or *Parsifal* or *Zarathustra* to have been left
unfinished.'

W. H. Auden, writing in *The New Republic*, begins by
decrying the fact that Kafka belongs to the cultists and ends
by discussing him with metaphysical hair-splitting in the
typical manner of the cultists, at a time when Kafka needed
a few blunt statements from appreciative sources. Auden has
written one of the most interesting and self-revealing statements of the philosophical problems in Kafka and has offered
suggestive literary hints, particularly in reference to the problem of the Quest. He sees Kafka from the point of view of his
particular prejudice, one aspect of which is an insistence that
the true significance of a neurosis is teleological and that the
questions with which Kafka dealt have very little to do with
his relationship with his father. Auden sees in Kafka only what
he wishes to see, his own Quest, his own torment between
skepticism and a desire for faith. He sees in Kafka both more

[18]

and less than the rational reader. Auden's eagerness to have Kafka on his side leads him to assume that Kafka belongs among the anti- or supernaturalists.

In the last analysis one may legitimately approach any artistic work solipsistically. But Kafka's appeal is not limited to mystical minds. Since his intended meanings have been obscured by his untimely death, and since a rational interpretation sounds just as cohesive and related as the mystical, it is legitimate to examine the mystical view from the vantage point of naturalism. The naturalist approach has the advantages of intelligibility, closer relation to the facts of biography and literary method, and, above all, closer relation to the world that created Kafka. As Stephen Spender wrote, Kafka is not interested in discovering a metaphysic but in penetrating reality to discover a system of truth.

As for the psychoanalytical (or perhaps it should be termed the Freudian-materialist) school, possibly its most prominent member in America is Harry Slochower, who, while he has written on other topics with admirable insight and logic, in his approach to Kafka is psychoanalytical to the extent that he tends to develop his thesis associationally rather than logically. His essay 'Franz Kafka: Pre-Fascist Exile' is illuminating, however, despite this handicap. It is particularly good in dealing with Kafka's social background and in the relation of the three novels (*Amerika*, *The Trial*, and *The Castle*) to the varying times that produced them. It is unfortunate, therefore, that Slochower is often guilty of such irrelevant statements, which muddy the waters so sorely in need of purification, as the following: 'The negative, repressive form of the sex act is the characteristic of Franz Kafka's writings.' 'The motif of sinning against the world of the Fathers is further symbolized by Karl's loss of his father's trunk when he lands in the new world. According to Stekel, luggage is "the burden of sin by which one is oppressed." ' 'In

Freud, the number three is symbolic of the male genitalia.' (This last in reference to the fact that in *The Trial* Joseph K. is led away to his execution by two men, one on each side of him.) 'Thomas Mann's Castorp, similarly suffering from lack of air (*there is even the parallel of the k-sound in his name*), "resolves" his dilemma by physical action on a communal battlefield.' (The italics are mine.)

In relating the novels to the times that produced them, Slochower maintains that between *Amerika* and *The Castle* Kafka grew progressively mature and therefore progressively gloomy. He calls *Amerika* Kafka's 'pre-war dream of a free country,' a dream shattered by the First World War, and proceeds to build up his case. Now this case, while laudable and unquestionably true in part, achieves error through false stress. As valid a case can be constructed on the basis of the literary mechanism. One can say, for example, that Kafka was feeling his literary way in *Amerika* and that therefore it is not as rich an expression of his tortuous, questioning dream-world as are *The Trial* and *The Castle.* He was sounding out his theme and still depending, to a considerable extent, on conventional realism for his effects. Later, when he mastered style and theme, he was able to achieve greater individuality and therefore originality. It is not only possible but quite probable that *The Trial* and *The Castle* would have been written without the First World War and its aftermath because their creation was dependent not so much on large-scale social events as on Kafka's inner torment, which, moreover, found expression not in ordinary realistic documentation but through allegory. The basic psychology of our century may have been deepened by the war but it was not created or challenged by it. The war was a symptom, not a cause. Thus Slochower is sometimes guilty of over-simplification on the social level and obscurantism on the psychoanalytic.

Also guilty along similar lines, is the Marxist critic, Edwin

Berry Burgum, in his otherwise comprehensive essay, 'Franz Kafka and the Bankruptcy of Faith.' He makes such unfounded assertions as the following: '. . . his attempt to escape a dominating father left his adolescence stranded upon the fluctuating shoals of the Weimar Republic'; 'his own diseased personality symbolized the disease at the heart of German society'; 'he takes us into the personality structure itself, remaining unconscious of its nature since he shares it'; 'since Kafka's last stories are almost exclusively devoted to his hallucinations'; 'that Kafka's anxieties have passed the norm and become psychotic in "The Burrow" is obvious'; 'this rare example ['The Burrow'] of successful communication of psychotic content'; 'K.'s murder symbolizes the final ascendancy of fascism. . .'

Burgum makes a great point of the influence of the Weimar Republic on Kafka's works; but the Republic was not established until the end of the war, when Kafka was thirty-five and when he had only six years to live. Therefore when Burgum speaks of the inefficiency of the Weimar Republic and of the effect of its bureaucracy on Kafka and *The Trial*, he misuses his facts; it was the empire bureaucracy of feudalistic Austria which bred Kafka, not the Weimar Republic. Burgum claims that Kafka grew progressively psychotic together with German society. But his elaborate analysis does not convince because he fails to explain how it was, if Kafka grew progressively psychotic (in fact as well as his fiction), that in his last years, in the words of Max Brod, 'his whole life took an unforeseen turn for the better, a new, happy, and positive turn which cancelled out his self-hatred and Nihilism.' Certainly there was nothing in the ominous growth of fascism (to use Burgum's own method) to warrant Kafka's new optimism and happiness. Burgum, unfortunately, never mentions these last years. His weakness, like Slochower's, is his too-great dependence on social reference frames in explaining

Kafka and his works. Such an interpretation is as basically misleading as the implication of the mystics that Kafka was not at all influenced by the problems of his time.

Another Marxist critic, Philip Rahv, in two otherwise illuminating essays, fluctuates between cerebration and intuition, picking up most of the mystical baggage of his predecessors and only occasionally, and then faint-heartedly, permitting an intuitive suspicion that Kafka was a rationalist after all. In 'The Hero as Lonely Man' he says outright that Kafka is 'the most genuine mystic in modern literature' and adds: 'The relationship of Kafka to K. is dramatic: within the latter he isolates his own rationalism for the purpose of purging himself of its impiety.' Thus he contradicts an earlier statement in the same essay:

The application of Freudian ideas to literature has often been gratuitous, but in Kafka's case it seems to me quite necessary. He is a writer who cannot be explained adequately by a strictly literary analysis, in terms of his literary qualities alone —and the methods of Freud are superior, I think, to the metaphysical flights which he has inspired in his German critics.

That is, although Rahv uses the methods of rationalism in exploring Kafka, he begins with the fallacious assumption that Kafka himself is not rational.

This first essay of Rahv's is, however, more cautious than his second, 'The Death of Ivan Ilyich and Joseph K.,' in which he swallows the mystical line almost completely, speaking of the tendency in The Trial 'against rationalism, against civilization, against the heresies of the man of the city whose penalty is spiritual death' and speaking of Kafka's 'all-absorbing belief in the incommensurability of the human and divine orders.' He proceeds in the following mystical manner:

But from the chrysalis of the Kafkian self there also emerges another figure, who, by means of a psychic transformation. assumes the role of judge and avenger. This dread antagonist summarily lifts K. out of his rationalist sloth and plunges the metaphysical knife into his breast. However, this antagonist is not a character we can recognize, he is not a living actor in the drama of K.'s fate. He is, rather, a transcendental emanation taking shape in the actual plot against K.'s life—and, in the final analysis, against the human faith in visible reality.

He goes even further:

He, the perverted modern man, can never adapt himself to the conditions of the absolute; he commits the most ludicrous errors and, though guilty, he thinks himself innocent. As he enters the Court he feels stifled in its pure air; its magnificent chambers he mistakes for dingy tenement rooms. Blinded by the fierce light of Moira, he can never experience the unity of justice and necessity, but must ever divide one from the other.

Near the conclusion of the essay, however, Rahv experiences a moment of doubt: 'Yet from another standpoint is it not possible to say that, objectively, Tolstoy and Kafka were really protesting against the irrational masquerading as the rational?'

In the second essay Rahv explores the so-called parallelism between the deaths of Ivan Ilyich and Joseph K., asserting that their authors punished them for their rationalism and typicality by torturing them with unknown afflictions, preparing them for death by arousing their consciences and then executing them. This thesis is interesting but it contains several errors of fact, the most important of which are: (1) While it is true that Ivan Ilyich's conscience is aroused by his impending death, Joseph K.'s conscience is already aroused when the novel opens—Ivan Ilyich is smug and self-assured in the beginning, while Joseph K. is uneasy and suffers guilt feelings always. (2) Whereas Ivan Ilyich is typical, Joseph K. is distinctly not so—it is precisely his atypicality which ruins him, for instead of being adjusted and accepting his

[23]

situation he insists on questioning and fighting 'the system.' (3) As for the types of rationalism of the two protagonists, which Rahv equates, Ivan Ilyich is an irrational character who calls upon rationalism (in the form of science and doctors) only when he is in trouble, while rationalism, skepticism, and, above all, integrity are the very bases of Joseph K.'s existence.

Certain aspects of the cabalas have become the common property of all the schools. What a furor, for example, has resulted from the fact that in *The Trial* and *The Castle* the heroes are anonymous. '*Amerika* is the only novel in which the hero *has a name*,' says Slochower. Elsewhere he says, 'The initial "K." suggests the stifling element in his life. Like the anonymous and standardized people in the expressionistic works, Kafka's unheroic hero lacks a name.' And Klaus Mann, in his preface to *Amerika*, says: 'Both of these remain strangely anonymous—or rather, they hide their mysterious identity with the author behind the obvious initial "K." . . .' Max Lerner, writing in the *Saturday Review of Literature*, cautions: '. . . note the progressive attenuation of the name.' And Burgum writes of *Amerika*, 'Its hero, Karl Rossman, is the only one among his writings to whom Kafka gave a name. The others are unnamed or generalized into "K."' And Estrada says: '. . . their individuality, generally recognized by physiognomy or name . . . is here reduced to a mere initial letter. . .'

Now it happens that Brod explicitly states, in a note to the English edition of *The Castle*, that the novel 'seems to have been begun as a story in the first person, the earlier chapters being altered by the author, "K." being inserted everywhere in place of "I," and the later chapters written straight out in the third person.' And in his epilogue to the English edition of *The Trial*, Brod reports that in his preparation of the manuscript he transcribed in full 'the innumerable contractions (for instance, instead of F.B., Fräulein Bürstner;

instead of T., Titorelli. . .' We have here, I think, sufficient information regarding the manuscripts to enable us to judge for ourselves whether the excitement is justified or whether it is simply another aspect of the cabala. We see that Kafka was in the habit of identifying his characters by their initials (probably for economy of time and effort), and that he identified himself, at least in an earlier stage of the work, with the K. of *The Castle*. Furthermore, there is the element of tradition in the use of abbreviation. At various times during the last century it was fashionable to write in the following manner: 'On the morning of the 16th day of May 18—, I came upon P—— in the town of Y——.' Incidentally, Kafka is hardly unique in his methods. Numerous authors have used abbreviations in their early drafts and some writers, prominent among them Dostoyevsky, have employed real names to help call the models to mind, just as Kafka used the initial of his surname to aid him in identifying his protagonists with himself. (It is also interesting to note that the F.B. in the manuscript of *The Trial* corresponds to the F.B. to whom Kafka was twice engaged.) All this indicates the possibility—one could even say the probability—that had Kafka lived to arrange for the publication of his last two novels he would have given his protagonists fictitious names, just as he did in works published during his lifetime.

The Irrational as Cabala

IT has been seen that the shortcomings of much of the literature on Kafka stem from too specialized views, from a lack of an understanding of the underlying issues in the Kafka quarrel, from a neglect of the 'merely' literary, and from the failure to see the Kafka details as parts of a whole, including biography, sociology, philosophy, and literary art. It remains now to indicate what has been missed in the Kafka search.

The irrational is a great motif in Kafka. Not only do his books suggest overpoweringly the irrationality of existence and its dominance over reason, but their basic fiber is the irrationality of dream-logic. He deals with the irrational not only as the container but also as the thing contained—his very approach to his truth is through the irrational. He does not look down into the irrational, as did the literary precursors of Freud, but up from it. It is to the discredit of the surrealists that they descend into disorder to wallow there, using the license granted by the new awareness of the unconscious, while it is Kafka's distinction that, caught in the web of disorder, he desperately and courageously seeks order, at the cost of his life. To him disorder is sin, it is a bohemia from which he would flee in terror, yet he suffers it, studies and catalogues it for the benefit of light and health. The surrealists wend an easy and shallow way to hell and beat their breasts in exultation half-way before arriving, convinced they have arrived. Theirs is the thrill of schoolboy sin. Kafka, however, is too familiar with sin, disorder, and disease to find them amusing or tolerable; he collects and codifies only for the ascent to the world. The surrealists are playboys let loose in a clinic, while Kafka is rabbi and doctor, Talmudist and scientific skeptic in one.

He is forever plagued by the irrational. First there is the dilemma of existence, the confused and blurred glimpse of the universe vouchsafed to man, the knowledge of death plus the ignorance of its meaning. Then there is the irrationality of society, the absence of reason in an age that calls itself enlightened, the operation of maxims such as might is right as witnessed in the continued force of national sovereignty, and individual possession of portions of the earth's crust. And finally there is the irrationality of the individual, of Kafka himself, with his monstrous torments and impulses. Often Kafka seems to be trying to show that there is no absolute truth, that truth depends on the point of view and that points of view cancel each other. Life, in short, is a torturous enigma. His work, too, in reproducing life as he knows it, is enigmatic.

To people who have sat on American juries, much of the argumentative and caviling aspect of Kafka will be familiar —particularly if they have sat on one of those numerous and typical civil cases where both sides present absolutely contradictory assertions and witnesses and where it is almost always impossible to decide rationally where the truth is, since the truth depends on the credibility of the witnesses and the varying points of view. A verdict in these cases is usually brought in on the basis of 'intuition' or 'faith' in regard to who is telling the truth. So it is in Kafka, where contradictory cases are elaborately developed concerning simple and seemingly obvious incidents and where no 'absolute' truth is ever achieved. This is the legal tone, the heritage of Kafka's law studies; and it is also his Talmudic heritage. In this connection it is apparent that the Hebraic tradition in Kafka is overwhelmingly stronger than the Hellenistic; the sensuous element in him is meager compared to the moral and intellectual. One feels that he is ashamed of the sensuous as if it were pagan and amoral. There is little of the musical in him, and little of the usual literary ornamentation.

Kafka is plagued, for he cannot allow irrationality; no matter how he strives to do so, no matter what mental gymnastics he attempts, he bluntly fails. Kierkegaard in the end is no solace, nor is the Kabbala, nor the mid-European mysticism of his friends. Therefore he despairs—of understanding his father, family, society, of realizing himself, of marrying—and so on endlessly; and his despair is forever heightened by his illness. There are men who learn to accept the irrational, but Kafka was too Talmudic and too modern for that. He was too thoroughly grounded in the Hebraic virtues of morality, order, and restraint to permit himself the Dionysiac luxury of abiding the irrational. If one may use Arnold's terms loosely, one may say that the nineteenth century was Hellenistic, with emphasis on the individual and the sensuous, and that the twentieth is Hebraic, with emphasis on the moral and the political. Kafka was caught in a trap between the two. A possible reason for his Talmudic leanings is that he was the epitome of minority—he was a Jew, intellectually raffiné, diseased. It is the minority that seeks safety in law and reason; and his being in a minority was Kafka's curse.

This extreme isolation is best expressed in Kafka by the use of the number two, by duality, the glaring opposite of singularity. It is two as completion, the opposite of aloneness. There are two assistants, the two inns, and the two sisters in *The Castle;* the two warders at the beginning and the two executioners at the end of *The Trial;* the two mechanics (Robinson and Delamarche) in *Amerika;* the two bouncing

[28]

balls, two girls, and two assistants in 'Blumfeld, An Elderly Bachelor'; the two young female assistants in 'My Neighbor'; the two horses in 'The Country Doctor,' etc. (I have counted 33 separate uses of the number two in *Amerika*, 51 in *The Trial*, 44 in *The Castle*, and many in the shorter fiction). An examination of the relation of Kafka's protagonists to the two is quite illuminating. The two, which stand for the norm, for society, are invariably irrational and rather mad from the point of view of the protagonists, who use utmost logic upon them in an effort at communication but who invariably fail. The protagonists feel superior to the foolish pair and yet they realize that the pair have a strength they themselves noticeably lack and yearn for—they have company, they have each other. The two are always presented as so similar in behavior as to be taken as identical twins. Who can be better adjusted than such twins, who are conscious of no singularity, each of whom possesses a perfect compatriot and comrade? Psychological studies have made this amply clear and no doubt Kafka understood this intuitively. A question arises: Why is it that he chose identical twins to represent unity and completion rather than the more conventional and widespread symbol of mates? Can it be that he preferred a homosexual completion to a heterosexual one? The known facts are insufficient to make a conclusion. We know, of course, that Kafka described sex relations in his novels—yet he always presented them as awkward and abortive; women are more truly mothers and comrades than mistresses. We know too that Kafka had affairs with women; yet he was incapable of bringing himself to marry. He broke off an engagement in panic at the last moment and once charged his father with having made him incapable of marriage. Is it possible that a father complex predisposed him to homosexual relations for basically psychic reasons? And is this the key to the narcissistic tone of all his writings?

[29]

In short, perhaps what Slochower calls the onanistic feature of Kafka's work is in reality the homosexual.

To Kafka, cabalism meant the secretive and superficial. When he spoke smilingly and enigmatically of 'a secret cabala' in his works he referred, in my opinion, to an attack on social cabalism, an attack savage and tenacious, as well as to a secret allegory. His friends and critics, however, have generally accepted his words at face value, mainly because they were impressed by his interest in Kierkegaard, his study of the Kabbala, and by his genuinely shy, poetic and 'religious' nature; and they have proceeded to split hairs upon chimerical foundations almost as deliriously as the court and castle functionaries in Kafka's major works. But they have failed to reckon with his profound skepticism and his fondness for the enigmatic; also his training as a lawyer and his ability to build up sound-seeming cases at the same time that he was secretly tearing them down. It is strange how certain critics strive to find philosophers in artists and artists in philosophers. Kafka is a man primarily of intuitions, emotions, and images—an artist—who presented more vividly than anyone else certain aspects of his experience common to his age.

Kafka in his fiction projected his personal deficiencies upon the society which seemed deliberately to exclude him; it was a way of striking back. There is evidence that he was aware of this projection and suspicious of it, and that at times he felt that society was justified in its treatment of him and that he and not it was evil. Perhaps it was for this reason that he asked Brod to destroy his unpublished works, thus renouncing them and thereby acknowledging the justification of society's case against him. From this point of view it is clear that his works may have induced great guilt feelings in him, just as his assertions before his father did. In a sense his works were aggressive acts, to be followed, in the neurotic pattern, by self-abasement. According to Brod, Kafka com-

[30]

plained that 'what he had already written, not to say published, led him astray in his further work,' which may account
for his reluctance to publish his work in his lifetime.

Kafka's works are an assault upon the reader; he deliberately teases and mystifies; it is his aggression at play. At the
same time they are a kind of hara-kiri on the doorstep of
society; only, and paradoxically, he lives to regret them. They
are the final insult as well as the final self-abasement; and they
are a romantic wooing by the mutant of the norm, the romantic self-slaying for the unobtainable beloved in the manner of
Werther. And always there is the symbolic commingling of
society and the Father, the rejection by the healthy and authoritarian. The key is Kafka's neurotic and trapped ambivalence, his hypochondriacal perversity which makes him
incapable of leaving his wound alone, which makes him probe
it masochistically with never-ending pain and delight, which
makes him value the wound as a sign of difference and
heightened and heightening spirituality, proudly exposing
it while ashamed of it.

'In how many conversations,' Brod has written, 'I tried to
make my friend see . . . his over-estimation of his father, the
senselessness of his self-distrust. It was entirely useless, the
flood of arguments with which Kafka defended his stand (if he
did not prefer to say nothing) left me shaken and at a loss.'
And again: 'This need [for his father's approval] was a fact,
an irrefutable feeling. It continued to affect Kafka to the end
as "the general burden of fear, weakness, and self-distrust." '
And yet the supernaturalists do not realize that Kafka's writings are extremely autobiographical. 'I had lost my self-
confidence with you, and exchanged a boundless sense of guilt
for it,' Kafka wrote his father. 'Remembering this boundless-
ness, I once wrote fittingly about someone: "He fears that his
feeling of shame may even survive him." ' This last refers to

[31]

the concluding words of *The Trial*. A man writes a highly neurotic and amazingly lengthy and complex 'letter' to his father at the age of thirty-six and still the mystics refuse to admit that Kafka's feelings toward his father were dominant in his thought and work and that his work is secular in meaning. They refuse to admit this even though Kafka said, in the letter, that he wanted to group everything he wrote under the collective title of *The Attempt to Escape from Father*. Brod lightly passes over this, commenting '. . . as if his love of art, his creative joy had not existed in its own right and strength,' forgetting, apparently, that the attempt to escape from the father and creative joy are not necessarily mutually exclusive or contradictory.

His *Letter to My Father,* one of Kafka's most revealing works, much of which has been suppressed by Brod 'for reasons of a personal nature,' contributes importantly to the understanding of cabalism as Kafka's basic theme. Kafka says to his father: 'For me you began to have that mysterious quality which all tyrants have, whose privilege is based on their personality, and not on reason,' and this is what he meant by the laws of the nobles, the court, the castle, and all the other symbols of outdated shibboleths that he presented. In addition to the bureaucracy under which he lived and the reactionary laws promulgated by the aristocracy, Kafka had another and perhaps most important example of cabalism in his immediate family life—in the Judaism of his father, which included a vast amount of flummery, such as chants and readings in the synagogue in a language few understood and symbolic manipulation of items that had ceased to have a vital significance thousands of years ago. Kafka wrote to his father:

. . . I failed to understand how you, with that mere nothing of Judaism you could muster, could criticize me for not exerting myself (at least out of respect for tradition, as you put it) to achieve a similar nothing. . . You went to synagogue on four days of the year; there you were, to say the least, closer to the indifferent ones than to those who took it seriously. . .

Kafka goes on at length, speaking derisively of the ceremony of the Bar Mitzvah as 'a silly memory test' and of the first Seder night as 'a farce with spasms of giggling.' He adds: 'And it was impossible to convince a child, over-observant from excessive fear, that the few trifling rituals you observed in the name of Judaism, with an indifference corresponding to their emptiness, could have a higher meaning.'

It is a mistake to suppose that Kafka in his writings is primarily the intellectual or that the intellectual element is the source of his inspiration. The intellectual is only a symbol and a vessel. Even if we grant that Brod is correct in saying that Kafka wrote of the incommensurability between the Absolute, between God, and the human, this in itself does not explain the passionate return to the wound, nor is it a fruitful concept to one so steeped in skepticism. After all, if the two are incommensurable, what can be done about it, what more can be said? But to Kafka's neurotic torment it is a perfect dilemma on the horns of which he may impale himself with remarkable variation. His reaction is neurotic, out of proportion to the stimulus. Kafka is diseased and this is the source of his inspiration, as it is in Dostoyevsky, Nietzsche, Schiller, and Novalis.

One can hardly blame society for reacting as it did to Kafka or as he imagined it did, for society, the 'norm,' must protect itself against the mutant, the genius, which it occasionally thrusts up. In the proud artistic revolt so characteristic of the nineteenth century it was fashionable to scorn society, yet secretly to envy and woo it, and in many cases rebellious artists who nevertheless wished admittance paid for their entry by creating works of beauty and nobility, often even while attacking society. But in Kafka's case he created in fiction, by projection, only the dubious paradoxes that plagued him, offering no token as a plea for peace and grace, and it may well be that these very acts of aggression drove him further from adjustment, so that in his last years, when he cancelled out his former nihilism, as Brod has said, and achieved an easier frame of mind, he wanted to destroy the unpublished works which lay heavy on his conscience.

At times Kafka seems to equate cabalism with society in general and at times to limit it to the irrational excesses of society that result in widespread suffering. But his basic attack is against unnecessary suffering—not the suffering of existence itself and the tragedy of life culminating in death—but that entailed by man's relations with his fellows. There is enough suffering in that we *are*, Kafka says, in that we lead a blind existence upon a planet spinning blindly into nowhere among millions of stars and planets; there is enough suffering in that —let us at least recognize that we are making a trip together and arrange it as pleasantly for each other as we can. Kafka is appalled by the blindness of his fellows, who, stoutly refusing to recognize that life is a tragic journey, will not see the value of acting decently on it. Such acute consciousness, such awareness of the basic element of suffering in highly reflective life, is typical of all reflective men who suffer bitterly, either from personal tragedy or from a feeling of alienation. It is the *Weltschmerz* of the romantic. In the case of Kafka it is heightened by his Hebraic-Slavic morality. And it is in his moral tone that he is superior to most of the other expressionists, many of whom found the art form a game of irresponsibility and delighted in its element of incommunicability, which is too often merely an excuse to shock the bourgeois.

In Kafka the personal tragedy was mingled with the sense of alienation—he was both a tubercular and a Jew; and in addition he suffered from a neurotic relationship with his father. It is easy, from these, to understand the psychology of

[34]

the outcast which he developed and presented. Because of these he understood the plight of minority groups, particularly of the oppressed; he understood how the oppressed slowly come to think themselves guilty and monstrous under the powerful and unrelieved suggestion of the oppressors. What gave him the insight was his apartness—to be apart is to question, while to belong is to be able to act irrationally without guilt pangs, provided the action conforms to the social conscience. 'I had always questioned myself over every trifle; in every trifle you convinced me, by your example and by the way you brought me up . . . of my incapability,' wrote Kafka to his father, speaking also of his 'nerve-destroying fear and sense of guilt.'

To be apart is to question; and to be thrown upon oneself means to have to create one's own conscience and therefore to seesaw between the criminal and the over-ethical, both of these, like conscience itself, relative factors differing widely in varying cultures. Man is so gregarious by nature that to be set apart entails a strong sense of guilt; retaliation is possible on the non-criminal level by superior reason and insight. The criminal and the over-ethical: the first defies the society from which one is an outcast, and the second both woos and attacks it with superior reason and morality. The over-ethical suggests the over-scrupulous, the psychoneurotic—and we know from Brod how scrupulous Kafka was. And from his work we are aware of the other element, the criminal, in the horrible, the monstrous, the outrageous in his work. The over-scrupulous suggests, in turn, perfectionism. May it not be that Kafka's literary perfectionism was an aspect of his neurosis? A perfectionism that urges one to destroy one's work and to be ashamed of it despite the assurances of objective critics is certainly abnormal; and perfectionist personalities are generally recognized as psychoneurotic.

To question: that is Hamlet's burden and an enormous

[35]

one. How much easier, safer, to belong. In this sense Kafka's theme is the incommensurability between the genius and society or the genius and the cabalism. Still he realizes that forms of behavior are necessary, for life is too complex for us to act scrupulously and consciously all the time, weighing each action on the basis of reason and 'absolute' justice. We require conditioning to face the business of living. The problem is: how to prevent a divorce between the form and the spirit of the cabala. The form without the spirit is obviously evil—it entails indifference to suffering, venality in administering justice, all under the pretense of spirit while the spirit is dead. It is good, therefore, to have mutants, the maladjusted like Kafka, to attack them from without.

It is interesting to note that the philosophy of naturalism stands in relation to anti-naturalism or supernaturalism as Kafka does to cabalism. For naturalism wishes to examine social myths or cabalisms from the point of view of evidence and reason and to define and categorize so that it is possible to determine when a myth is form without spirit—in short, to promote the better life within the capability and dignity of man.

In *The Trial*, cabalism is epitomized by the law and the court, by their irrational, unjust, and deliberately clandestine and capricious nature, which places the burden of proof on the accused, then leads him from one psychological trap into another, and by a process of alternating encouragement and discouragement enervates him until he is ready to accept spiritual execution. But the court could not exist without a general belief in its existence and power. Therefore the people, who support the mores and effect the social pressures, are a party to the continuation of the cabalism. Kafka is not an anarchist decrying governments or bureaucracies, but he is indeed decrying their unjust elements. Hans Christian Andersen would have adults experience a revelation because of a child's insight; Kafka would have the adults hound the child until it too believes, against the evidence of its fresh senses, that the emperor is clothed. In a fairy tale the hero conquers obstacles until he lives happily ever after; in Kafka obstacles conquer the hero until he dies or lives miserably ever after. Kafka's devices are basically quite capable of inversion. It would be easy enough to make most of his works pleasant fairy tales with happy endings simply by making the obstacles inspire the heroes to new confidence and strength. Kafka's fable in *The Trial* as well as in the rest of his work is the education of all youthful idealists into adjusted middle-aged 'realists.' The escape from the court is belief in oneself, in one's integrity, one's senses, and one's logic. This belief, plus the courage of aggressiveness, will avoid disaster.

A similar satire on cabalism permeates *The Castle*, only there the accused is an entire group, the Barnabas family. In *The Trial* social pressures are presented directly in only one instance, in Joseph K.'s uncle's attitude toward K., while all others are stated indirectly or hinted at. In *The Castle* the various forms of pressure are described in detail, such a procedure being consonant with the author's new purpose: an examination of the communal aspects of his theme.

This interpretation of Kafka may also be applied theologically, not in a mystical sense of personal revelation but rather in the sense of faith in God, which inevitably means faith in the eventual triumph of goodness and order in man. In such an application it would appear that religious bureaucracy is the cabalism, that one needs no advocate to plead one's case with God, that God can be reached only by direct and simple communion, and that the door to God is always open. All one needs is the courage to disregard the hocus-pocus of the doorkeeper and to pass through. The cathedral in *The Trial*, with its verger, priest, and barbaric ornamentation, emphasizes Kafka's conception of organized religion as a cabalism. It is significant that the priest calls himself the prison chaplain and that he and the cathedral are instruments of the court, which is to say that the church is playing secular power politics. K. is supposed to show an Italian around the cathedral—suggesting Romanism or the extreme of religious orthodoxy. All the window blinds around the cathedral square are commonly drawn, an indication that the cathedral is remote from the people, that it has no vital relation to their lives. This notion of religion as cabalism may or may not have been one aspect of what Kafka meant, although it seems likely. In any case it has relevance, particularly if one is inclined to equate the concept of God with justice based on reason. It seems apparent that the inclusion of this point as a possibility in no way invalidates my disagreement with the mystical interpretation, since my point of difference still hinges on the concept of God and the divine.

The essence of both Kafka's portrayal of cabalism and his ironic and implied comment on it can be found in the final chapter of *The Trial* in Joseph K.'s conversation with the priest in the cathedral. The latter encourages the confused K. with his tale of the doorkeeper and the law, giving him the clue for his salvation, but when K. leaps at the suggestion the priest, who is a court functionary, immediately proceeds to smother him in a fog of Jesuitical and Talmudic quibbling, further confusing K., who all along has been filled with feelings of inferiority and guilt and therefore has not been able to trust his intuitions against the mumbo-jumbo of authority. In this final confusion K. completely accepts his fate, so that later, when he is being led to his death by his two executioners (who, incidentally, have not been given definite orders relating to their task and are apparently instruments of K.'s will rather than of the court's), K., on coming upon a policeman in the street, a man who might help him, actually sprints away, carrying his executioners with him. But just before his death he is again ambivalent, this time bitterly so; however, by now his will has been sapped and he is destroyed. Kafka's use of the cathedral and the priest relates his theme here more closely than elsewhere to religion but again not in the sense of mystical revelation—rather of faith in one's intuition, logic, and sense of justice.

Kafka's attitude toward cabalisms is revealed in these insights in Brod's biography:

In all things Kafka came in touch with, he sought that which was significant, rooted in the world of truth. . . His attitude ignored completely all literary hierarchies, ranks and classifications. Everywhere he grasped essentials. . . He was prejudiced neither into accepting nor into rejecting a general opinion on principle. The refreshing thing about him was the absence of any preoccupation with paradox. He was, in fact, preoccupied by its antithesis. His judgment had an elementary simplicity, naturalness and obviousness; it was easy and sure in spite of the caution with which he gave it, and the willingness, the almost passionate willingness with which he admitted error.

Yet Brod writes, in his note to *The Castle*: 'The essential thing to be noted is that the hero in *The Trial* is persecuted by an invisible and mysterious authority and summoned to stand his trial, and that in *The Castle* he is prevented from doing exactly the same thing.' This is a misreading of the facts that has been accepted by many critics who have simply picked it up from Brod. (It is unfortunate, for example, that Thomas Mann has lent his considerable influence to the mystical theory in his introduction to the American edition of *The Castle*. It should be noted, however, that his conception of the divine is sharply at variance with Muir's and somewhat

[39]

with Brod's; his God is conceived in terms of the human.) *
Joseph K. stands trial not because he is summoned but only
because he believes in the accusation and in his basic guilt,
unproved as these may be; he is never forced to stand trial.
And the K. of *The Castle* is not prevented from standing trial
by anything except his own timidity and his own willingness,
despite his being a stranger with perspective, to accept the
nonsensical cabala that the castle is powerful 'and unapproach-
able. In both instances the cause of the plot development lies
in the protagonists themselves. Brod fails to understand this,
probably because he does not have sufficient perspective on
European super-respect for authority and tradition, something
that Kafka attained only through his fantastic sense of isolation.

One can agree that K.'s efforts to become a member of
the village community represent a search for grace, for acceptance, but one cannot agree that the castle represents either
the dispensation of grace or the divine. In not one instance
does the castle manifest real power; its power is purely suggestive, it resides only in the superstitions of the villagers; in
this sense it is similar to the court of *The Trial*. Only the
villagers can dispense grace, only they can accept or ostracize.
Therefore the irony of the novel, as well as the implied criticism of the 'divine' school, lies in the fact that K.'s sole
possibility for grace rests in himself, in his willingness to
become like the villagers in order to be accepted by them, in
his readiness to accept the village superstitions, the castle
cabalism. In short, he must give up his dependence on justice
related to logic. Obviously this is not what Kafka advocated;
therefore the book can be read only as a satire on what he did

---

* In answer to this Thomas Mann wrote me: 'Concerning my own
occasional utterance about Kafka, I did not really want to classify him
with the mystics when I characterized him as a "religious humorist."
Religious allusion and symbolism cannot be denied in his works, particularly in *The Trial* and *The Castle*, but for a mystic even his style is
too clear and rational.'

not advocate, a satire on the particular search for grace that K. represents. This the mystical school does not see, since it is blinded, by its obsession with the castle as the divine, into as ready an acceptance of the castle cabalism as that of the villagers. The mystical interpreters, in short, manage to adjust themselves very nicely to the village; and it is they who find the state of grace, not K. Nor does the fact that Kafka yearned to belong controvert my explanation. At the same time that he yearned to belong he despised belonging.

Muir's nebulous note in *The Castle* is simply a rationalization of Brod's categories of divine law and divine grace. In it he contradicts Mann by saying that Kafka 'avoided scrupulously the pose of the spectacular wrestler with God.' Mann, in the same volume, says of *The Castle*, 'It is the most patient, obstinate, desperate "wrestling with the angel" that ever happened. . .' Muir's short note is replete with such nonsense as the following: 'While following the adventures of his heroes we seem to be discovering—almost without being fully aware of it—various things about those entities, divine powers, which we had never divined before, and could never perhaps have divined by ourselves.'

The story, 'Investigations of a Dog,' which is perhaps Kafka's last work, is also one of his most explicit. Here the symbolism is least involved and opaque and the tone and content most confessional. It is as if the tired and very ill Kafka is writing his last testament—not in the complicated and dramatic manner of the novels but rather in an essayistic mood, although still within a limited framework of expressionism. For these reasons and because he kept repeating his themes it is extremely enlightening regarding Kafka's meaning. The mystics, however, must postulate the existence of the nonexistent to explain Kafka in their terms. Thus Muir writes, in the introduction to *The Great Wall of China*: 'To understand it properly one must assume that the human race are invisible

[41]

though still operatively present, roughly fulfilling towards the dog world the role of divine and incomprehensible powers.' This sort of approach might well have assumed the existence of an invisible but 'operatively present' moon between us and our visible one to explain the discrepancies in Newton's gravitational theory. But from the rational, naturalist point of view, no such postulation as Muir's is necessary—one is required only to look facts in the face and weigh the evidence in a manner that is generally and rationally verifiable.

Note the essayistic and autobiographical elements in the beginning of the story. The protagonist dog, which I shall call the K-dog from now on, is queer, yet not exempt from the laws of his species: '. . . somewhat cold, reserved, shy and calculating, but all things considered a normal enough dog.' The K-dog makes an ironic commentary on non-dog species (including man):

But one thing is too obvious to have escaped me; namely, how little inclined they are, compared with us dogs, to stick together, how silently and unfamiliarly and with what a curious hostility they pass each other by, how mean are the interests that suffice to bind them together for a little in ostensible union, and how often these very interests give rise to hatred and conflict.

As for dogs:

We are drawn to each other and nothing can prevent us from satisfying that communal impulse; all our laws and institutions, the few that I still know and the many that I have forgotten, go back to this longing for the greatest bliss we are capable of, the warm comfort of being together. But now consider the other side of the picture. . .

And the K-dog shows how dogs are separated from each other by 'distinctions of class, of kind, of occupation, distinctions too numerous to review at a glance. . .' Then he cries out against himself because he cannot live as the others, accepting in silence whatever disturbs the harmony—that is, the divisive forces.

Soon the K-dog describes a remarkable experience in his youth which set him upon his endless investigations—the meeting with the seven 'musical' dogs. The important elements of the incident are (a) whenever the K-dog is skeptical or critical or curious about the behavior of the seven, he is instantly knocked flat by their music, in short he is conditioned against skepticism, criticism, and curiosity, and (b) the seven are compulsive in their behavior or forced into it for some reason unknown to the K-dog. The reason is the irrational cabalism. The K-dog cannot understand the cause or meaning of the horrible music and he longs to shout to the seven and to beg them to enlighten him—but before he can speak the violent music flagellates him mercilessly. At first the K-dog is impressed by the courage of the seven and their power to endure the music calmly but on closer study he sees it is not calmness that characterizes the seven as much as extreme tension. In short, they are not behaving naturally but are following a pattern imposed on them. Why are they afraid, the K-dog wonders and he shouts out questions, but the seven carefully pay no attention to the innocent mutant. Then the K-dog notices that the seven 'had flung away all shame' and were walking on their hind legs—were acting like humans. Inverted (and inversion here, as in Butler's *Erewhon* and Swift's *Gulliver's Travels,* is a satiric device) this reads: humans acting like animals, crawling on all fours. The K-dog tries to keep them from committing further sin but the music again overpowers him—that is, the cabalism cudgels him.

Talmudic rationalizations of the incident from contradictory points of view follow in the usual Kafka manner. Later the K-dog inquires into the question: What does the canine race nourish itself upon? He accepts certain facts relating to the question and is happy to agree with the majority in this. 'Quite honestly I have no ambition to be peculiar, or to pose as being in the right against the majority; I am only too happy when I can agree with my comrades, as I do in this case.' But, not content, he goes still further and asks where the earth finds the food it thrusts up, a tabooed question that usually elicits the answer, 'If you haven't enough to eat, we'll give you some of ours.' The reaction to this question is twofold: on the one hand dogs find it stupid; yet they are attracted to it—the attraction of the norm for the genius mingled with the fear of him.

It becomes increasingly clear that what the K-dog wants admitted is the knowledge of the basic tragedy of life—this would be some consolation for his alienation and a point of comradeship between him and the others—as well as the basic irrationality of cabalistic behavior and the lack of reason and originality of the devotees. But he meets only silence. Finally he says of his kind:

We are the dogs who are crushed by the silence, who long to break through it, literally to get a breath of fresh air; the others seem to thrive on silence: true, that is only so in appearance, as in the case of the musical dogs, who ostensibly were quite calm when they played, but in reality were in a state of intense excitement. . .

To the mystical school I can offer only the rebuke of Zeus to man in the *Odyssey*: 'Lo, you now, how vainly mortal men do blame the gods! For of us they say comes evil, whereas they even of themselves through the blindness of their own hearts, have sorrows beyond that which is ordained.'

This might well stand as the motto over Kafka's works.

This view—in terms of cabalism—of Kafka's life and work is so central to both that it illuminates even structural or formalistic difficulties in his major works (let alone his minor) which otherwise cannot be dealt with intelligently or at best must be discussed in the jargon of mysticism and what-not. The difficulties throw light, in their turn, upon Kafka's essential meaning. For form is indissoluble from meaning in genuine artistic works; they cannot properly be examined one without the other. Let me then discuss one of the most enlightening as well as puzzling structural discrepancies in Kafka—the structural difference between the tightly knit *Trial* and the loose, rambling *Castle*.

In *The Trial* one notes a wealth of subjectivism and is fascinated by the dream-distortion technique, the irrational and neurotic, which are intimately revealed through the mind and reactions of Joseph K. These features are responsible for the novel's impact, its drama, and its experiential value. But one looks for them quite often in vain in *The Castle*, at any rate until the major and key chapter, fifteen, in which Olga relates her story to K. While Kafka was interested in the K. of *The Trial* as an individual he was interested in the K. of *The Castle* as a device with which to view the village. In *The Trial* he was concerned with individual psychology in relation to his theme, in *The Castle* with communal psychology. Only by making these distinctions between Kafka's purposes in these two novels can one avoid falling into the error of regarding Joseph K. and K. as identical heroes. The hero of *The Castle* analogous to Joseph K. is the Barnabas family, which suffered extremely unpleasant relations with the castle and the village. Between this family and Joseph K. there is a real affinity. The Barnabas family, like Joseph K., is convinced of its guilt; they worry not about the absolute state of things but only about the fact that misfortune befell *them*. As for K., he is the hero as outsider, used by the author to bring perspective and skepticism to bear upon the hypnotized people of the village. In this sense he is similar to Hans Castorp in *The Magic Mountain* and Tchitchikov in *Dead Souls*.

[45]

The nature of Kafka's reaction to the cabalism of his day may perhaps be seen most clearly when viewed in the perspective furnished by a contrast between Kafka and the nineteenth-century Samuel Butler, another victim and antagonist of cabalism. In order to clear the ground for an examination of the striking similarities in their lives and work, let us first acknowledge their very real differences.

Butler's tendencies were toward science and rationalism, Kafka's toward philosophy and art. Butler was a rather arid character who haunted the British Museum and worried about posterity's appraisal of him. Kafka was feminine, poetic, chaotic, and was so little concerned about posterity that he failed to finish his three major works and requested that they be burned after his death. Butler was the product of nineteenth-century formalism; Kafka was a typical twentieth-century character: neurotic and ironical and full of outward as well as inward turmoil. Butler had only a thin love for the accepted masters of art and for art in general, caring very little for the German masters, for example, with the exception of Handel. Occasionally he sneered at Goethe and Beethoven (he distrusted the romantics and suspected anyone with a large reputation). Kafka loved the romantics and revered Goethe. Butler belonged to the British world of science and materialism and flourishing empire of the nineteenth century, while Kafka's world was the decadent, outmoded, bureaucratic and feudalistic world of pre-war Austria, a world writhing with psychoanalysis and mysticism in revolt against the extremes to which nineteenth-century rationalism had gone.

Yet in spite of these differences their patterns are basically similar. Butler barely escaped the life of a churchman, Kafka that of a lawyer. The church plays a large role in Butler's works and the law in Kafka's. Both men hungered for acceptance by the cabalisms of their times and both were rejected. Both, in consequence, retaliated through their works, and in doing so reproduced the cabalisms in order to satirize them. In the process they portrayed the essence of cabalas with such a ring of truth and at the same time so ambivalently and allusively that they seemed to have created cabalas of their own when in reality they were merely giving vent to the scorn and bitterness of their rejection. The cabalisms they attacked were dissimilar—Butler lashed out at the cabalism of scientific professionalism and smug professionalism in general; Kafka at the social, ethical and philosophical cabalism best symbolized for him by the bureaucracy with which he was so disastrously familiar. The causes of their attacks were approximately the same: father-troubles resulting in feelings of inferiority, in the psychology of the outcast, which lent them the fresh view of the stranger pressing his nose against the window of contemporary life. Butler's attack was for the most part rationalistic (he was an island of rationalism in the romantic stream of nineteenth-century English literature), while Kafka's was psychological. As for the more apparent similarities, both were lifelong and neurotic bachelors, both suffered from father complexes, both were ridden by feelings of guilt and inferiority, both had their major work published posthumously, and both were the products of authoritarianism which found expression in the father. Butler, the product of Victorian rigidity and arrogance, revolted openly against his father and made his final and most exhaustive attack on him in *The Way of All Flesh*. Kafka, the product of Austrian feudalism, of a bureaucratic, paperwork empire, revolted negatively by withdrawing into a shell of pain and developing anxiety and guilt. Apparently Butler's father was more susceptible to direct attack than Kafka's, for he cut a rather ludicrous figure with his excessive discipline mixed with extreme sentimentality. On the other hand, Kafka's father stood in Franz's eyes, for a long time, as the personification of extroverted success and acceptance of and by the world.

[47]

In the works themselves there are numerous and fertile centers of comparison. To mention only one, there is the similarity between Butler's *Erewhon* and *Erewhon Revisited,* and Kafka's *The Trial* and *The Castle.* Butler comments on the problems of his day through the medium of fantasy, in which he has an excellent opportunity to display his love of intellectual perversity, of turning things inside out. The two books are reminiscent of *Gulliver's Travels* in their caustic and shrewd examination of society. Kafka also uses fantasy to examine society and to exercise his love of *emotional* perversity. Thus he handles the subjective element of criticism, for in a sense he is more interested in effect than cause, being primarily an artist rather than a thinker like Butler.

One often has the feeling in Kafka that he is describing the spiritual state of the majority of people, their slavery to fad, attitude, tradition. His great social truth is acceptance of cabalism—e.g. of the might and isolation of the castle and the existence and authority of the court. Even K., the outsider, never asks Olga the direct question and the only meaningful one: Why hasn't she gone to the castle directly and in person to plead her family's case? K. himself gives up trying to reach the castle directly after one minor attempt, thereafter losing himself in a morass of indirection. But basic questions are, of course, forbidden in a cabala. And so how true is Kafka's portrayal of the process of pyramiding rationalization upon rationalization in the ceaseless and shrewd explanations that give the effect of actuality to the baseless and the nonexistent. In this sense his works form a skeptical spiritual fable of modern man. In his view, modern man is a neurotic with a sapped will, which is a matter of a bad conscience and social insecurity. His exemplifications of the physical results of mental conditions, in such characters as Block in *The Trial* and Olga's father in *The Castle*, are in line with the conceptions of psychosomatic medicine.

When the student carries off the law-court attendant's wife to the latter's obvious pleasure in *The Trial*, Joseph K. slowly follows them and realizes that this is his first unequivocal defeat from these people attached to the court. But he tells himself that he received the defeat only because he insisted on giving battle. 'While he stayed quietly at home and went about his ordinary vocations he remained superior to all these people and could clear any of them out of his path with a hearty kick,' says Kafka. This is one of the purest dramatizations of Kafka's guilt motif. K. suffers a defeat because he gives battle; he gives battle because of a heavy sense of guilt which urges him to defend himself against a baseless charge; he feels this guilt because of his overdeveloped conscience; his conscience is the result of his sensitivity; and his sensitivity, inevitably, has been overstimulated by the injustice everywhere evident in society. K. could have avoided defeat by denying his guilt, by staying at home, in other words by looking the other way in the face of injustice, by stifling his conscience.

It becomes apparent that K. is not simply a neurotic who defends himself against any charge, no matter how foolish; he is also, because of his own suffering, a man of compassion with a fine regard for the rights of others. And so he is, on the one hand, a tormented Don Quixote tilting with windmills of his own creation, and on the other a neurotic genius who insists on fighting his case with logic and conscience. He is a genius despite his neurosis and because of his strange methods; and yet in the end he suffers the unnecessary fate of all the accused because of his neurosis: he is executed—symbolically by two men but psychologically by himself. He is not able to tear out of his mind the hypnotic web of guilt and accusation which subtly strangles him; he is the victim of auto-suggestion.

What are we to deduce from this? We can deduce that neurosis is a societal as well as a personal phenomenon and that society must be held responsible for it. We can also deduce that the remedy for a man like K., who is after all a typical specimen, is to free himself of his neurosis either by himself, beginning by defying any hints of auto-suggestion, or with professional help. But his cure must not lead simply to an ability to scorn baseless accusations but also to a defiance of the social structures that create the neuroses which in turn incapacitate those of sensitivity and conscience to deal with the structures. In other words, it is not enough for him to emerge as the normal citizen with the latter's normal callousness in political affairs; he must, because of his greater vision and compassion, defend the rights of all men by attacking the political and economic, the reactionary cabalas which stifle man's development. He must emerge as the unneurotic genius.

Kafka, for all his modernity of manner and technique, is a psychological primitive in the same sense that Freud is, giving new meaning to adulthood by exploring the layers of childhood that adhere. But he is not a primitive in anything approaching the anthropological meaning, of course; his characters are, rather, highly civilized people who, like modern man in general, are profoundly childlike. Kafka seems to be reminding us that childhood and dreams are closely related, dreams being childish and childhood dreamlike. And he seems to be recalling that Western man's constantly greater understanding and appreciation of childhood, of both its beauties and its terrors, has followed his development since the Renaissance. Clearly as man develops horizontally in broadening his world view he also, because of his increasing feeling of isolation in a mechanistic and power-mad society, extends himself vertically in his psychology for better and for worse, reaching down into the wells of dream, childhood, and myth. In his artistic exploitation of these motifs Kafka is the descendant of

Schopenhauer, who was among the earliest thinkers to emphasize the power of the unconscious. Unlike Dostoyevsky, who is a master of abnormal psychology in adults, and Henry James, Marcel Proust, and Thomas Mann, who are masters of societal psychological subtleties, Kafka is a master of the psychology of the dream: the irrational, distorted, and primitive. And while the psychology of the trio is highly societal even when individualized, Kafka is extremely individual even when socialized. He stands, because of his psychology, in the romantic tradition despite his classic style; while such a novelist as Proust, on the other hand, remains a classicist for all his stylistic eccentricities.

One of Kafka's basic themes is none other than the one so prevalent in his time and so rich in blood-brothers both before and after—the portrait of the artist as outcast. If in Kafka's case the outcast seems also to be a psychoneurotic, it is only because of his greater isolation. Like Thomas Mann's early artistic protagonists (especially Tonio Kröger), Kafka's heroes yearn for identification and acceptance by the 'regular' and the 'normal,' the extrovertive pillars of society. This is clear throughout Kafka's work and is particularly explicit in 'Investigations of a Dog,' as we have seen. This theme in Kafka is to be viewed, therefore, as part of a well-traveled stream rather than as some isolated rivulet; his use of expressionism rather than impressionism or realism should not be permitted to obscure this point. Expressionism, which came into favor in certain quarters as a reaction to the deadening photographic quality of an over-exploited realism, served Kafka's needs well. Lacking the aggressiveness of a James Joyce, who could strike back at the regular in no uncertain terms through Stephen Dedalus, Kafka found the new form an adequate veil of modesty to cover his spiritual disrobing. Touches of realism he employed only to keep his autobiography from soaring altogether into the realm of incommunicable fantasy, spicing the result with symbolism for artistic effect as well as intelligibility. Thus, beginning more extremely than Joyce in medium, he did not go as far as Joyce's quasi-schizophrenic meanderings; on the contrary, his effects grew increasingly explicit. As for Mann, who picked up realism at its point of perfection, he saved himself from enslavement to it by the use of symbolism and musical devices. Mann is the type of writer, like Goethe and Tolstoy, who writes autobiographically and who builds around an emotion or an idea; that is, he externalizes. Kafka, like all sick geniuses, internalizes, writing in the language of the wound itself; he does not try to exorcise the pain by verbalizing it; on the contrary he prolongs it excruciatingly, encouraging it to breed new pain. If Kafka at times crosses over into the psychopathic in his work, it does not follow that he himself is psychopathic. It is well known that the psychoneurotic has psychotic tendencies. All that can be said is that at times Kafka gives vent to these tendencies, sublimating them; the biographical facts are too clear to allow any other assertion.

Kafka's books are full of marvelous externalized psychology as well as inner psychology. It is this psychology which is his forte, for after all his intellectual message is negligible and his qualities as a man dealing with beauty are negligible too. But his bits of psychological business are truly remarkable; together with his dream-method they create a lasting effect. This effect is proof of the broad base of his theme and method. While reading him we are impressed by the feeling that the world as we know it, like Kafka's dream-suggestions, is largely irrational; in other words, living in an irrational world is like living in a dream, with all the uncertainties, frustrations, and fears of the latter. But quite often Kafka's people are abnormal, so that sometimes one wonders whether his novels are studies in the psychology of failure and paranoia: how is it, then, that the reader can identify himself

[52]

with them? The answer is that we, even in our 'normality,' being the products of our society, are, like Kafka, basically neurotic: driven, anxious, inhibited. This fact, together with Kafka's powers of evocation, makes him one of the most effective modern practitioners of the literature of catharsis.

Of the many aspects of neurosis, Kafka stresses one the understanding of which came late in the history of psychiatry: that delicate neurotic balance between loving and hating oneself, between protecting and destroying oneself, which often has its predominant expression in the form of severe masochism. Straightforward masochism is mainly interesting from a medical point of view; it lacks the drama of conflict and ambivalence found in more subtle forms. It is, therefore, the latter that Kafka treats so tellingly in his novels, in those twilight states of mind in which the will to protect barely flickers before the choking will to destroy oneself. This powerful urge to destroy oneself is the inner villain of Kafka's novels, the outer being the court and the castle—or the cabalism—which are largely responsible for the urge. Masochism is obviously an expression of one's feelings of worthlessness, which in severe cases is cultivated for the pleasure it offers as sheer feeling. In Kafka's case this feeling stemmed from his comparison of himself with his father as well as his consciousness of his irregularity in society. His father is the outer but absent villain of the novels, the inner being Kafka himself, or at any rate his excessive sensitivity or attenuation, which deprived him of the normal aggressiveness necessary to assert himself before his father's ego. For Kafka his father was a personification of the cabalism of his day.

The other side of the coin of masochism is sadism, and both are the poles of the neurotic's ambivalence. Kafka seems to be saying that sadism is equivalent, in democracies, to the free-for-all quest for success and power which allows the devil to take the hindmost and which encourages everyone to step on the face of the man beneath him on the ladder; in the monarchic, semi-feudalistic countries such as Austria it is equivalent to the existence of the rigid autocracy which sits as legislator as well as judge over the people, averting its eyes from the sight of mass suffering and degradation.

It is Kafka's distinction that he realized the universal implications of his exaggerated sense of guilt and that he was able to apply this realization to a penetrating evocation of the ramifications of guilt in modern man. Is there, then, a great residue of guilt in us all and does our age differ from others in this respect? In most other times the categories of behaving and thinking were more strictly drawn and bounded; it was therefore easier to know the 'right' way of life. Today everything is fluid and ambivalent, the 'right' way far from certain. Compromise is the general rule, compromise between 'idealism' and 'realism,' compromise which, in sensitive persons who already share the general neurosis of the age, leads to profound feelings of guilt. Someone once said that irony is the factor that differentiates the twentieth century mind from all others. That touches the problem but does not explore it. For what is the cause of this irony? It is based on the dualism and ambivalence which are the result of the interplay of a heightened skepticism with a heightened idealism, the result of a struggle between a more firm vision of the ideal, particularly of the social ideal, with a growing despair of achieving it. There is another approach. If irony is the philosophic or artistic result of the struggle, what is the psychological? A sense of guilt. Greater knowledge, by its expansion of the conscience, involves the possibility of greater sin. Therefore a sense of guilt and ambivalence are characteristic of our time. And Franz Kafka is unique because he perceived these facts so completely on the imaginative, emotional, poetic planes, giving us, through his conscious dreams, a more intense and complete and above all experiential awareness of these factors in ourselves.

Kafka is basically a poet—in terms of imagination, conception, and meaning—despite his medium. He sinks his shafts deeply into the unconscious, fetching up symbols that are often erotically evocative, like those in dreams. His debt to dream life is incalculable; this is not accidental, for he was aware of dreams acutely and in addition possessed an unusually fertile and vivid dream life. In his diaries he describes dreams in great length and detail, in absolutely coherent prose and with no little literary merit.

It is extraordinary how he manages to balance himself between chaos and reason; this extends an enormous tension to his situations and his prose. It would be easy to fall into complete distortion, into automatic writing, into the thoroughly undisciplined; but Kafka remains disciplined in the midst of his disorder. His tact and taste invariably save him; and what are these but his absolute skepticism, his unwillingness to indulge in sentimentality either of the realistic or surrealistic variety? With this in mind his insistence on the use of conventional, 'classic' prose is understandable and commendable.

Kafka's long paragraphs, running on at times without regard for dialogue or change of pace or mood, at first puzzle and annoy, but soon one realizes that their effect is not, as in Proust and Mann, that of density and architectural solidity but rather that of breathlessness. This quality is typical of Kafka and is also a feature of the German expressionist school; but it is only one facet; indiscrimination is another; together they create a kind of wonderful buzzing in the reader's ear, which suggests irony, irrationality, and dissonance—or, if you will, the modern temper.

In certain nightmares we experience the torment of being unable to flee in the face of danger; this is a recurring motif in Kafka. The feet of his protagonists are likely to stick and their bodies grow sluggish precisely when their anxiety is at its height. This feeling of hysteria also occurs in serious illness, which brings to mind the thought that much of Kafka can be described as the psychology of disease—the helplessness, the incomprehension of the healthy, the distortion, the inaccessibility, the narcissism, the dependence. Almost invariably characters act toward Kafka's protagonists as nurses toward invalids, somewhat patronizingly, with an excessive show of health and with a certain obliviousness to suffering. All of which recalls Kafka's neurasthenia, frailty, and tuberculosis. The explicit absence of air in many of Kafka's situations can be viewed as an objectification of his actual condition—of his neurotic breathlessness, also of his chest awareness as a tubercular.

The world of Franz Kafka is sometimes reminiscent of Hemingway because of its sadism, but Kafka's sadists are never Hemingwayish outlaws; as a matter of fact there is no element of the lawless in the sense of 'wild' in all of Kafka. The most refined cruelties are part of some established program; the atmosphere is closed in, one is weighed down by the sense of tradition, there is a palpable heaviness of spirit in the air. It is the stale air of Europe, of course. Even the humor is a little desperate; everything is desperate, everything trembles with exaggeration; the healthy is a little too healthy. One feels that the books could easily have been written by a Japanese, in a land exhausted by topheavy and bloodless tradition.

The world of Franz Kafka. . . It *is* a world, consistent and rare, the inspiration genuine; the nether world, the lower depths of the spirit, where the deepest truths, the hidden truths, reside, from which they move the puppets of the upper regions. It is a world of sustained visions; Kafka was able to plunge into the creative unconscious and remain with his muse in that breathless twilight longer than most.

Strange: he who was an expert at rejection, who rejected even himself as a human being and at times rejected the notion that he possessed talent, by his example restated the truth of

[56]

the maxim that greatness can be attained only by being oneself. In his writings he finally accepted himself, accepted the
ugly and tormented duckling, accepted the sick, irrational, and
castoff, all elements of his remarkable world; and by so doing
reached the rare atmosphere of universal truths which stands
above the cabalisms in which his feet were enmeshed; here he
belonged, here he breathed at last, with the noblest and the
best, the pure uncompromising air of art and truth.

Portrait of an Artist as Pariah

FRANZ KAFKA was born in Prague 3 July 1883. He was the eldest of six children. His two brothers, Heinrich and George, died in their infancy, the first at two, the second at a year and a half, leaving Franz the sole male child among three unfriendly females. Franz at an early age met death not as something vague in the upstairs world of adults, but as an awful gap evidencing the quicksandish nature of life. The trauma may have in large part been responsible for his early pessimism and later psychic onanism. He already suffered from being the eldest child, with all the difficulties of adjustment that this fact classically implies. Besides, he was a male in a highly patriarchal society, the son of a striving burgher casting hungry eyes about for a capable heir. He came up early against his father's disappointment. To be deprived of two sons and spared a weakling, an eccentric taking after the mother's side: this must have been a blow for the father. Franz, flung down and trampled upon by massive unknown forces, began to revolve like a satellite around his sun-god father, transfixed by the glow that both warmed and consumed him. Seeking an attacker, he found one ready-made.

Tall, powerful, ambitious, the son of a butcher in Wossek, in South Bohemia, Franz's father was one of six children whom his mother described as giants. After a hard youth, he was intent on making things comfortable for himself and his family. Sometimes, on relaxing at home in the evening—he ran a prosperous wholesale warehouse in the Old Town Square, stocking haberdashery for sale to retailers in villages and country towns—he would expand with tales of his early life, hinting at the soft life of his children, a practice that often set Franz's teeth on edge. On the father's side were physical strength and endurance. Franz's grandfather 'could lift a sack of flour from the ground with his teeth,' according to Brod.

On the mother's side were pious men, scholars, ascetics, dreamers, freaks, many of whom died young. Franz's great-grandfather on his mother's side 'used to bathe in the river every day, even in winter, when he would cut a hole in the ice to bathe in,' Kafka once noted in his diary. Kafka himself wore thin clothing in freezing weather, was a fresh-air and nature enthusiast, and at one time a vegetarian.

Like Thomas Mann, he experienced a parental dialectic whose effects were profound in his life and work, his father representing the bourgeois and nature, his mother the bohemian and spirit. But whereas Mann assumed the appurtenances of burgherdom in his personal life while toying with the illicit in his work, balancing himself precariously while attempting a Hegelian synthesis, Kafka's hypochondriacal asceticism and scrupulosity prevented him from playing the good burgher with any lasting success.

Kafka's childhood was lonely, apprehensive, and depressing. The boy, convinced he was unsightly, feared new clothes because he thought they emphasized his ugliness, and he was afraid of mirrors for the same reason. According to his mother, he was a 'weak, delicate child, generally serious, but nevertheless ready for an occasional prank—a child who read a lot, and didn't want to take any exercise.' He attended the German elementary school in the Fleischmarkt and later the German grammar school in the Old Town Square. He was brought up as a German and went to German schools exclusively. Later he acquired a knowledge of Czech and 'a deep understanding of its literature.'

Many critics have underestimated the Czech element in Kafka's work, thinking of him romantically as *creatio ex nihilo* or as some sort of *Luftmensch,* one without roots, who lives in the air and off of it. Kafka's work has its roots deep in Czech tradition, especially in the joys and sorrows of Prague and Bohemia. One of his important themes is the problem of authority. Almost invariably authority is portrayed as absolute. For this conception he had ample inspiration. The sadness of the Czechs for three centuries was the result of their defeat by the Hapsburgs at the Battle of the White Mountain (*Bílá hora*) on 8 November 1620, and their consequent systematic oppression by the reactionary, absolutist, Catholic Empire. Bismarck succinctly said that he who was master of Bohemia was master of Europe. Bohemia traditionally has been the battleground between Slavic and Teutonic forces, between Protestantism and Catholicism, between an indigenous enlightenment and medieval reaction, between mysticism and rationalism and, in the final analysis, between romanticism and an outworn classicism.

The Czechs have known oppression from the receiving end and in the finest variations. Long before *Bílá hora,* Dalimil, a chronicler, wrote:

> Shed no tears for him, my children,
> But know, I pray you, only this:
> Had this your prince ruled o'er you longer
> Then had our land more evil wars.

He was referring to Rudolf, the first Hapsburg to sit on the Bohemian throne, a regent who died in less than a year of his reign while on an expedition against some rebellious Czech nobles. Kafka's almost religious passion for truth is an echo of John Huss's motto, which was: 'Seek the truth, know the truth, respect the truth, hold the truth unto death.' Huss once wrote, 'Truth vanquishes all, for he who is being killed for the sake of truth gains victory.' He was burned at the stake for his leadership in the Reformation, having to the end refused to recant.

It was Bohemia's misfortune to be conquered by a monarchy that for centuries constituted one of the most backward states in the economic and political structures of Europe, a state devoted to the antiquated feudal system and the absolute powers of the dynasty. The conquered land, down to the reigns of Maria Theresa and Joseph II, was given over to the military, to taxgatherers, and to Jesuits. The Hapsburgs banished the best of the nobility and the most valuable citizens—such as Comenius—and Germanized the country, outlawing the native tongue. Ferdinand II lost no time after *Bílá hora* in executing twenty-seven leaders of the Czech cause in front of the town hall on the Old Town Square and in issuing the *Erneuerte Landesordnung*, Revised Ordinance of the Land, which smashed the powers of the Czech nobility. The country was made a gift for the Counter-Reformation. The Jesuits were given charge of Prague University and the gymnasia, while the Piarists took over the lowest schools.

The influence of the Jesuits' casuistry, scholarship, and peripatetic philosophy is as evident in the works of Kafka as is the casuistry of the Talmud. At the beginning of the seventeenth century, after fifty years of Jesuit activity, Bohemia was still 90 per cent Protestant; but at the end of the eighteenth century it was almost completely Catholic under the Jesuit pressure. However, liberalism was welcome in Bohemia after the Counter-Reformation and apostasy from Catholicism was epidemic. At all times the simple people, the serfs and peasants, got the worst of the oppression. They responded with a surprising mixture of fatalism and rebellion akin to the spirit of the Russian peasants of the last century. In the meantime they nurtured the native language, safeguarding it until the beginning of the Czech national revival in the late eighteenth century. It was they who found the oppressive rule least comprehensible. Often enough they did not understand the language of the conquerors—the official language—a fact hinted at in Kafka's 'In the Penal Colony,' in which the condemned man, a peasant, does not know the charges against him or the sentence that has been passed by his superiors, since the elegant officer converses in 'French.'

Kafka's sympathy for the peasants is apparent in much of his work. On the other hand he despises the nobility and is tireless in selecting feudal symbols such as castle, manor, and armor to portray the oppressor and authority. With the bureaucracy and inhumanity of the Austro-Hungarian Empire he had intimate experience. All these he portrayed in his work, not directly but allusively, symbolically. The spirit of rebellion is in his work—rebellion against an autocratic, repressive church, against the feudalism of which he found evidence all around him, and against the absolutism of the conquerors.

Kafka's creative talents manifested themselves precociously. While still a child he wrote little plays for his sisters in celebration of his parents' birthdays. These were acted out, but Franz remained characteristically in the background as stage manager.

His appearance and behavior as a young man belied his inner turmoil. Tall, slim, observant, reserved, with a healthy laugh, he inspired a feeling of well-being in those around him, hiding his morbidity and emphasizing the healthy side of himself. Brod reports that 'he was brave, a good horseman, swimmer, and oarsman' and interested in 'every kind of reform—e.g. in the methods of natural healing, in modern methods of education, such as the Montessori system.' To know Kafka only from his books was to know him falsely, because of the marked contrast between his outer and inner lives, says Brod; he states that Kafka avoided the bizarre, had a strong social conscience and was 'a wonderfully helpful friend,' with a keen knowledge of the world. 'He was often late for appointments, not out of unpunctuality, but because he had felt the need to settle some other business absolutely before leaving it.' Absolute truthfulness was one of the most important and distinctive features of his character. 'He was extremely gentle and tolerant, rarely angry and rarely indulged in self-pity.' Some people found him charmingly naive—his employer referred to him as 'our office baby.' Others found round him a saintly aura.

He was unusually reticent about his work and its meaning. Brod was friendly with him for several years before he learned that he wrote. His literary tastes were catholic. For Meyrink he had no time, he could quote Hofmannsthal with admiration, he did not care for Wedekind or Oscar Wilde, but was enthusiastic about Hamsun, Hesse, Kassner, Hebel, Fontane, Stifter, Stefan George, Robert Walser, and the prose translation of Chinese lyrics by Heilmann, and above all Goethe, Flaubert, and the Bible. He loved Thomas Mann's *Tonio Kröger* and 'reverently searched out every line of this author's in *Die Neue Rundschau.*' In later years he liked Emil Strauss, Wilhelm Schäfer, and Carossa. He admired Dickens and Benjamin Franklin and much of Balzac. In the case of certain authors, such as Grillparzer and Hebbel, he preferred their diaries to their works. He felt an affinity with Kleist and was deeply influenced by his style. He read Kierkegaard with admiration.

In 1906 Kafka obtained his doctorate in jurisprudence and then did the usual unpaid so-called year in the courts, with no intention, however, of being called to the bar, since he hated the study of law and undertook it only because it seemed the least troublesome of the many subjects available.

He intended to enter the civil service. After a short prelude 'in the most strenuous of commercial offices' (the Assicurazioni Generali) he landed a longed-for job in 1908 with a semi-government office in Prague, the Workers' Accident Insurance Institute for the Kingdom of Bohemia. Such a job, in which work stopped at two each afternoon, was to be found mainly in government offices, and was not easy for Jews to obtain. Kafka felt himself lucky. Yet it was here that he was gorged with the knowledge of the red tape and callousness of bureaucracy, with maiming accidents and sudden death. His social conscience was stirred: 'How modest these men are,' he once said to Brod. 'They come to us and beg. Instead of storming the Institute and smashing it to little pieces, they come and beg.' His experiences at the Institute deepened his pessimism and heightened his awareness of the insubstantiality, insecurity, and disorder of life.

In 1909 Kafka read to Brod the beginning of a novel entitled *Preparations for a Wedding in the Country,* the manuscript of which survives in part. In 1910 he read him a long story, 'Description of a Battle.' Kafka was published for the first time when he was twenty-six, a section of the 'Description of a Battle' appearing in Franz Blei's journal, *Hyperion.* That same year, 1909, a semi-journalistic effort, 'The Airplanes at Brescia,' was published in a Prague daily, *Bohemia.* In 1910 several small sketches were included in the Easter supplement of the daily.

In the meantime Kafka's life was by no means compounded merely of the job and his writing. There were holidays in the country, walking tours, visits to Paris, Lugano, Weimar, Riva; friendships with Felix Weltsch, Oskar Baum, Martin Buber, Otto Pick, Willy Haas, Ernst Weiss, Rudolf Fuchs, Franz Werfel, and others; attendance at Czech mass meetings and debates; and interest in a Polish-Jewish troupe of actors who performed folk drama in Yiddish. From this troupe Kafka 'gained deep insight into the customs and spiritual crises of the Polish-Russian Jews.' He began to study Jewish history and the history of Jewish literature. There were also occasional trips to the opera and to concerts, mainly on Brod's instigation, for Kafka, says Brod, was notoriously unmusical. He once told Brod jokingly, but with a certain truth, that he couldn't tell the difference between *The Merry Widow* and *Tristan and Isolde*. After a Brahms concert Kafka wrote in his diary, 'Listening to music, by its nature, sets a wall around me, and the only lasting musical effect is that, shut in in this way, I am anything but free.'

Thus ended the first period of Kafka's life. The second began on 13 August 1912, when he met a young woman, F.B., at Brod's house, with whom he fell deeply in love. This period lasted for ten years, ending with *The Castle*. Woman for Kafka was the symbol and means of salvation, an escape from his father and therapy for himself. As a result, his meeting with F.B. had important consequences for his work. He experienced an artistic breakthrough a little more than a month after meeting her, discovering the theme and style characteristic of him. On the night of 22-3 September he composed the story 'The Verdict' in one sitting lasting all night. It was his first genuine story, with all the accoutrements of the genre, yet strikingly original. Kafka was ecstatic. He dedicated the piece to F.B., relating it on 29 September to Brod and Felix Weltsch (they had been away at Portorose) after going to the station to tell them of his breakthrough, a highly unusual procedure for the immaculately modest and reserved Kafka. The following year it appeared in Max Brod's annual, *Arcadia*. The style was the tortured and torturing expressionism; the theme, with rich variations, the quest for salvation through marriage and domesticity, the villain being the ubiquitous and terrifying father image.

The breakthrough was only a beginning. Kafka immediately began work on a novel entitled *The Man Who Disappeared, or Amerika.* On 6 October, he read to Brod both 'The Verdict' and 'The Stoker,' the latter the first chapter of *Amerika.* But by late October he was already troubled by his relations with F.B. He wrote her a twenty-two page letter and noted in his diary that he was worried about the future. On 3 November 1912 he read to Brod and Baum the second chapter of *Amerika.* Later that same month he read to them *The Metamorphosis.*

In January 1913 Kafka's first book appeared, *Contemplation,* a thin volume of impressionistic sketches, dedicated 'To M.B.' Kafka considered the pieces 'worthless fragments.' He had prepared the manuscript after much hesitation, from the wealth of papers of his diary. According to Brod, he was full of 'despair at his ignorance of the rules of spelling and punctuation.' In May 1913 'The Stoker' appeared as one of 'Der Jüngste Tag' series of small paperbound books published by Kurt Wolff in Leipzig. For this piece Kafka was awarded the Fontane Prize in 1915.

The next year was one of great tension for him because of his accelerated relations with F.B., yet his artistic inspiration did not lessen. He was full of plans and sketches and his diaries teemed with dreams, as if both his day and night lives were in ceaseless fermentation. Marriage for him was the great dilemma, the final salvation as well as the dreaded pit. That he was difficult to handle and that he was making F.B. miserable he himself recognized. As early as 9 November 1912, he had drafted a letter to her, warning her against him. At times she grew desperate and wanted to break off her relations with him. Whenever she did, he redoubled his efforts to keep her, as though without her he were finally lost. Yet at the same time he drew up lists for and against marriage, adding in large letters: 'Miserable me!' and 'What misery.' In the meantime a voluminous correspondence continued and Kafka blew hot and cold. In August 1913 he proposed to her, in September he wrote Brod: 'The very idea of a honeymoon fills me with horror.' He wrote from Riva, where he was on vacation from his problems and where he had an obscure affair with a Swiss girl. Finally, in May or June of 1914 he became officially engaged to F.B. in Berlin. But by the end of July he broke the engagement.

Brod believes that these 'terrible upheavals' were the inspiration of 'two new long works which were written after the breaking-off of the engagement'—*The Trial* and 'In the Penal Colony.' In September 1914 Kafka read Brod the first chapter of *The Trial* and in November 'In the Penal Colony.' In October he took a week's leave from his office 'to push the novel a bit,' prolonging the leave by a further week. On 13 December he finished the ninth chapter of *The Trial*, which he described as the 'Exegesis of the Legend.' On 18 December he wrote 'The Giant Mole,' which he left unfinished. During the Christmas holidays he read to Max Brod and the latter's wife the final chapter of *Amerika*.

The relationship with F.B. was by no means finished. Late in 1914 it was rejuvenated. Suddenly Kafka saw the brighter side of things—yet not quite. During this time he made efforts to become independent by moving out of his parents' home. In February 1915, at the age of almost 32, he finally removed himself from the spell of the family circle, renting a room. In April 1915 he read to Brod the fifth and sixth chapters of *The Trial*. In the meantime he suffered from severe headaches and sleeplessness, writing in his diary, 'Take me, take me, network that I am of madness and pain,' and reproaching himself, in his conduct toward F.B., with 'the office-clerk's vices of weakness, meanness, indecision, counting the cost, caution . . . the soul of a clerk, childishness, a will broken by my father. . .'

At this time he read Strindberg, the Bible, Dostoyevsky, Pascal, Herzen, and Kropotkin. In the winter of 1916-17 he lived in Alchemists' Street in a quiet room with a tiny kitchen and a loft, a place Brod describes in his diary as 'The monastic cell of a real writer.' Here Kafka wrote 'The Bucket Rider' during the coal shortage and made serious preparations for his coming marriage.

Then, in August, he coughed up blood. He insisted it was psychic in origin, something to save him from marriage, calling it his final defeat, and he refused to see a doctor. At the same time he began to sleep well. He was living in a flat that could not be heated and had been wearing the usual light clothing and going in for 'hygienic' measures. His father had warned him against 'extravagances' of this kind. By 4 September Brod managed, after constant entreaties, to persuade Kafka to visit a doctor. They went together. The verdict: catarrh in the lungs, with the danger of tuberculosis. A three-month rest was ordered. On 10 December Kafka and Brod visited the doctor again. A sanatorium for tubercular patients was suggested. Kafka refused. He went instead to Zürau, near Saaz, where his youngest sister managed the small estate of her brother-in-law. Here he came for the first time into close contact with country life. He began slowly to recover. But his relationship with F.B. was at an end. He last saw her in Prague during the Christmas holidays. One morning he came to Brod's busy office without warning, his face pale and severe, and suddenly began to weep, something Brod had never witnessed. He had just seen F.B. off on the train for the last time. Fifteen months later F.B. married. Kafka was moved, happy for her.

Kafka remained in Zürau until the summer of 1918, then returned to Prague and resumed his work at the office, spending his afternoons gardening in a suburb. He began to put together the manuscript of *The Country Doctor*, dedicating the book to his father. It appeared in the following year, together with 'In the Penal Colony.' In 1919 he lived for a few months in Schelesen near Liboch, in a boardinghouse, at first alone, then in the winter with Brod. There a second 'unhappy tale of love and betrothal' began, but it had a speedy end. Then in November 1919 Kafka wrote the hundred-page *Letter to My Father*. The letter was an attempt to clarify Kafka's conscience before his father, to assert his final independence, and to illumine their painful relationship from his point of view. It constitutes a short autobiography, brilliantly and movingly written.

Kafka's illness lingered on, despite all the good effects of his stay at Zürau. In 1920 he went to Meran, then to the Tatra Mountains in an effort to cure himself, but the illness was becoming more acute, sometimes bringing on severe crises. He coughed a good deal, suffered from fever and shortness of breath. On 15 March 1922 he read to Brod the beginning of *The Castle*. In October 'The Hunger-Artist' appeared in *Die Neue Rundschau*.

In the summer of 1923 Kafka was staying with his sister in Müritz on the Baltic. There he became interested in a holiday colony of the Berlin Jewish People's Home. One day he noticed a girl in the Home's kitchen, busily scaling fish. 'Such gentle hands, and such bloody work,' he commented. This was the beginning of his relationship with Dora Dymant, with whom he went to live in Berlin and who remained with him until his death. She was about nineteen or twenty, of a Polish orthodox Jewish family, intelligent and an excellent Hebrew scholar. Kafka was studying Hebrew at the time and was pleased with her knowledge of it. He seemed to experience a character transformation under her influence. He decided to cut all his ties with his family and to live with her in Berlin. This he did, leaving Prague at the end of July 1923.

They lived in the suburb of Steglitz, and Kafka was deliriously happy. He slept well, was optimistic—yet his health declined. He wrote 'A Little Woman,' 'The Burrow,'

'Investigations of a Dog.' The winter of the inflation set in and Kafka was tormented by the sufferings of the poor. He and Dora Dymant suffered from a shortage of coal and food. He fought against receiving help from his family in fear of losing his hard-won independence. By March 1924 his health failed so alarmingly that he had to return to Prague. He was sent to a Vienna clinic. From there he was moved to Kierling. Here he suffered great pain in his larynx. Both his larynx and lungs were now irreparably damaged by tuberculosis. Soon he was forbidden to speak much and he took to writing notes.

When it was too late, he wanted desperately to live. He followed the doctor's orders exactly and saw the hope of a new life for himself. Just before he died he said to the doctor who was attending him, while he was in great pain, 'Kill me, or else you are a murderer.' On 3 June 1924, a Tuesday, he died. On 11 June he was buried in the Jewish cemetery in Prague. His parents were later buried in the same grave.

iv

The Shorter Fiction

KAFKA's shorter fiction, with its tightness and sameness of mood, its dream atmosphere and its absence of precise characterization, bears the impress of his strange personality as thoroughly as do his novels. But the tales are usually more peripheral and less personal and suggestive than the novels. Whereas the novels are rooted in Kafka's father period, the tales span his entire creative life.

Kafka's first period, which ended on 13 August 1912, with his meeting with F.B., contains his exploratory efforts. This period is characterized by a lack of sustaining power, a search for original themes, and an inclination to impressionism. The dream-world of expressionism is present, adorned by the pastel smears of impressionism. The father motifs are almost wholly absent. The second period, during which Kafka realized himself thematically and achieved his distinctive style, owes its creative excellence to the emergence of the father crisis. All of the great works derive from the brief decade that lasted until late 1922. The final, two-year period is not of great importance. In it Kafka produced 'Investigations of a Dog,' 'The Burrow,' some of the minor tales of *The Great Wall of China,* and a few of the posthumous pieces.

'Description of a Battle,' a novella of about 13,000 words, differs from Kafka's later works in its lack of control, its un-

[71]

pleasant dithyrambic tone, and the narrow application of its theme. The theme—loneliness, frustration, cynicism—is handled personally rather than with the universal overtones of the mature works. Although the tale begins expressionistically it soon assumes a remarkable surrealist air, with supernatural activity added to the dream elements of expressionism. Portraying a world less stifled than Kafka's later world, it is surprisingly powerful. It contains, to an unusual degree in Kafka, nature phenomena beautifully described, and displays prominently an early use of the symbol two

Contemplation, a book of ninety-nine pages containing eighteen short pieces that made no pretense of being stories or even fiction, but which were simply bits of confessional literature, notes from a diary in dramatic and lyrical form, appeared when Kafka was almost thirty. The oddness of the project consisted in its size as well as in its subject matter. The author had delivered to the publisher so skimpy a manuscript that the latter was forced to use huge type, heavily leaded, and wide margins, in order to produce a book at all. The result resembled a primer for children. Kafka was almost completely unknown, yet his book, limited to an edition of 800 copies, established him in a special circle and gave him that impetus which only intelligent audiences can offer and without which the most self-sufficient artist is likely to suffer.

These early pieces, distinguished by an uncommon point of view, a marked genuineness of tone, and an unusually restrained and capable manner, are semi-impressionistic, revealing a powerful graphic sense lacking in the later Kafka. They illuminate a tender poetic side of the author seldom seen again. Their nostalgia is all the more moving because it is countered by the author's unflinching irony and his absolute independence of self-pity. Some of the pieces, such as 'Children of the Highway,' have a pastel quality rare in Kafka's bleached world. 'A Wish to be an Indian' is only a sentence long, yet it expresses adequately Kafka's neurotic desire for unrestraint. Already one hears his implied complaints against an environment that is weary and cluttered. The artist as rejected is a motif heard throughout, especially in 'The Refusal,' in which the beautiful girl who rejects the narrator's advances is a kind of blue-eyed creature out of Mann's *Tonio Kröger*.

From the beginning, it seems, Kafka spoke only to himself, without striving for effect or desiring to be eccentric. 'The Trees,' a sketch of a few lines, emphasizes his favorite notion of the world's illusoriness. His difficulty in making decisions because of his overscrupulousness is stated in 'The Runners.' His love of opposition is everywhere evident: desire *versus* boredom, motion *versus* stillness, nostalgia *versus* bitterness. Symbols that will be used widely and effectively later make their appearance: the number two, the pair, the candle. 'Being Unhappy' is the strangest sketch of the lot, resembling his later work in its emphasis on the absurd.

'The Verdict' is the first work that bears unequivocally Kafka's major literary traits—the nightmarish atmosphere, the hidden core of ramified personal allusion, the father-son conflict, and the symbolism of darkness, airlessness, and illness. Kafka jotted down in his diary on 11 February 1913 a few notes concerning this story.

I am taking advantage of the proofreading of 'The Verdict' to jot down, as far as I can remember them now, all the relationships that became clear to me during the course of the story. This is necessary, because the story came out of me like a real human birth, covered with dirt and slime, and I am the only person that has the hand that can reach the body itself, and that cares to do so. The friend is the link between father and son, he is the greatest thing they have in common. Sitting alone at his window, Georg takes a sensual pleasure in rooting about in this common possession, believes he has his father in himself and, but for a fleeting, sad hesitation, considers that everything is peaceful. The development of the story now shows how out of this common thing, the friend, the father comes to the foreground, and sets himself up as Georg's opposite, strengthened by other lesser common possessions, such as by the mother's love and devotion, by the loyal memory of her, and by the customers whom, it is true, the father originally cultivated for the sake of his business. Georg has nothing, the fiancée who lives in the story only through her relations with the friend, i.e., with the common possession, and who just because there has not yet been even a marriage, cannot enter into the blood bond that is drawn round the father and the son, is easily driven away by the father. The whole of what they have in common is built up on the father, Georg finds nothing in it but what is foreign, what has come to be taken for granted, something he has never sufficiently looked after, something exposed to Russian revolutions, and it is merely because he himself has nothing else save the sight of his father, that the verdict that shuts his father off from him completely has such a powerful effect on him.

Georg has the same number of letters as Franz. In Bendemann, the 'mann' is there only to strengthen the syllable 'Bende' [bonds] in case of any unforeseen possibilities in the story. But Bende has the same number of letters as Kafka, and the vowel 'e' is repeated in the same positions as the vowel 'a' in Kafka.

Frieda has exactly the same number of letters as F. and begins with the same letter; Brandenfeld begins with the same letter as B. . .

This diary excerpt suggests the ecstatic nature of Kafka's experience as well as the similarity of the tale's symbolism to actual facts. And it indicates Kafka's limited understanding of the tale's implications. When he says that the friend in Petersburg is the link between father and son, the greatest thing they have in common, he fails to see that he is also the essential point of difference between them. It is not true that Georg has nothing left save the sight of his father; on the contrary, he has everything; it is the father who has nothing.

[74]

Kafka saw the tale only as an undistorting mirror of reality. The story contains a series of reversals and a marriage of opposites. The father is idealized, he is interested in moral scruples and social decencies, he is a spiritual fellow in contrast with the real Kafka senior, the pushing philistine. The son is the philistine in the tale. Thus the fictional father is Franz and Georg, the fictional son, is Hermann Kafka. The friend in Petersburg is a composite of both figures. Like Franz he is an outsider; he wears a 'foreign' beard, he is unhappy, unsuccessful, a bachelor, 'innocent.' Like Hermann he is straightforward, independent, and a striver.

Georg is a pharisee, a fact which Kafka does not recognize. He is cruel to write to a lonely bachelor of his three engagements: 'Moreover, in my fiancée, who sends you sincere greetings and who will write you herself very soon, you will gain a candid friend, which is not wholly insignificant for a bachelor.' By pretending to be scrupulous about his friend's feelings, he manages to cut him off from any news of consequence. He has also been mistreating his father. His conscience pangs are identifiable with Kafka's. Kafka felt guilty because of his irregularity, frailty, and ambivalence. He wished to satisfy his father's demands of him, demands he resisted all the more strenuously because of his filial urge to fulfil them. To punish himself in the story, he disguises himself in the figure of Georg, the Babbitt. Thus one hand washes the other: while castigating his irregularity he also flagellates Babbittry in general and any traces of it in himself. Georg's wish to 'cover up' his father is symbolic of his desire to kill him. He is condemned to death because of it. He carries out the sentence only because he is suddenly overwhelmed by his guilt.

As for the Petersburg friend, he is a symbolic projection of Georg's better side, his Kafka nature. When Georg's father asks him whether he really has a friend in Petersburg he is not evidencing insanity, as some critics assert. He is playing a

[75]

game with Georg, implying: 'Have you really got that better side which you claim to have?' This hidden thrust sets off Georg's garrulous solicitations. 'Georg,' says the father softly, his head upon his breast, as if appealing to his son's conscience. Hard pressed, Georg undresses him and puts him to bed. Symbolically, Hermann Kafka challenges the existence of Franz's better self, as expressed by his aesthetic and intellectual interests, and accuses Franz of using it as a pretext to be parasitical. In rejecting his friend, Georg rejected his conscience. This is what the father accuses him of. 'Well do I know your friend,' he cries. 'He would be a son after my own heart. That's why you have deceived him all these years. Why else? Do you think I did not weep for him?' Georg is moved. 'The Petersburg friend whom his father suddenly knew so well affected him as never before. He saw him lost in distant Russia. He saw him at the door of his empty, plundered house. He still stood among the ruins of the bookcases, the tattered merchandise, the falling gas fixtures. Why did he have to go so far away?'

The use of opposites as censors is well known in the study of dream dynamics. The opposition and balance of emotional forces, a characteristic of Kafka's work, lends it that valuable quality of impartiality. Kafka's portrayal of the father as ill and decrepit is symptomatic of both his aggression and his guilt toward him. The more immediate autobiographical references are clearer still. Frieda Brandenfeld stands for F.B., as Kafka himself asserted. Kafka had known her about a month when he wrote the tale; this month appears as the time that Georg has been engaged. Kafka envisioned his father as standing in the way of his marriage. Georg's father therefore complains about his son's engagement, descends to vulgarity in referring to Georg's fiancée, and promises to sweep the girl from Georg's side. Significantly, Kafka dedicated the tale to F.B.

[76]

In *The Metamorphosis,* the most masochistic piece of his mature period, Kafka portrays himself as a gigantic bug which plagues a decent family. The autobiographical inferences are inescapable. The affair with F.B. released Kafka's pent-up masochism in the form of literary savagery and horror. An important motivation for the length of the novella must have been Kafka's creative momentum. This is clear from the essentially weak thematic development and powerful stylistic treatment, as if Kafka were carried off by his literary strength to effects beyond his thematic interest or sincerity. The novella is important as a tour de force that permitted Kafka to flex his literary muscles. As in 'The Verdict,' Kafka presents the protagonist as a philistine. But Gregor Samsa, unlike Georg, is an eminently good son; he is in fact fanatically good. And he is the economic mainstay of a parasitic family. This is a wish projection of a Kafka depressed by his economic dependence on his father. The tale is full of attacks upon the father. The device of reversal is clearly operative here too, although now moral or character reversal is replaced by a financial one.

The strength of the novella resides in its fertile invention and its power of empathy. It is not an 'amazing' story; it differs from most horror tales because of its core of immediate and personal truth, consisting especially of the universality of disaster and the fear of the unknown. One feels that the actual transformation is merely symbolic of more real and deadly transformations which are ever possible and which haunt even the healthiest and best-adjusted of beings. There is implicit everywhere the neurotic's horror of losing control, and there are hints of fear of the lower depths of sleep, night, and dream, and also of existence in death without the release of death—a mythical echo of Tantalus.

A few scattered points are worth mentioning. There is Kafka's method of convincing the reader by a *fait accompli;* he states in a casual manner: 'When Gregor Samsa awoke one morning from troubled dreams, he found himself changed into an enormous bug.' The illusion of transformation is achieved not only by a sort of bug documentation but also by the behavior of the parents and sister, who never forget that the bug is their Gregor. There is the verbal parallelism between Samsa and Kafka—even closer than between Bende and Kafka. There are the usual perspicacious psychosomatic implications, e.g. the gradual physical degeneration of the family under the impact of disaster, and their regeneration after Gregor's death. (A slip on Kafka's part, surprising in view of his meticulous care to preserve unity of point of view, is the break near the end of the tale. Kafka might have concluded with Gregor's expiration. He seems, however, to have been unwilling to forego the opportunity of a few more digs at the family's expense. He lovingly presents them as glorying in their sudden freedom.) And finally there is the constant and subtle use of the symbol two.

According to Brod, 'In the Penal Colony' was written shortly after Kafka's first break with F.B., in July 1914. It is thus a companion piece of *The Trial*. Brod says, with justification, that both of these works are masochistic, 'documents of literary self-punishment, imaginative treatment of sins.' A distinction should be made, however, between the two works, inasmuch as in *The Trial* the protagonist is the victim of violence whereas in 'In the Penal Colony' he is an observer. The tale has the same relation to Kafka's shorter fiction that the novel has to *Amerika* and *The Castle*. It reflects a broadening of theme and a depersonalizing tendency; the autobiographical element and the father motif are spiritualized into a larger social context. In 'In the Penal Colony' Kafka for the first time in his short fiction introduces and attacks the notion of the social cabala, transforming the conception of authority from the father-image level to the level of society as father.

The officer and his machine represent an outmoded social

system. The officer, who prides himself on his daintiness and sense of honor, while lacking any humanitarian impulses, is a feudalistic robot. He is interested, to the exclusion of almost everything else, and with absolute indifference to the feelings and fate of the condemned man, in the smooth operation of the machine. The condemned peasant has been ordered to die for a mere technicality. He is given no opportunity to defend himself. The officer cannot tolerate the possibility of the man's innocence; to permit the man to defend himself would only obscure the issue. His code, with its cruelty, its personal honor, and its inclusion of suicide as an escape, is Prussianistic. Kafka was not unaware in depicting the social drama that preceded the First World War.

The new governor is humanitarian. With the support of the explorer he is certain to defeat the remnants of the old guard. The aristocratic machine, like the torture machine, falls to pieces. The death of the officer is accompanied by ritual—he neatly breaks his sword; but he is desecrated, the machine does not handle him with refinement; it does not torture him subtly, it simply murders him outright. For the military mind this is the difference between a firing squad and hanging. The explorer is the outsider with perspective. Throughout, the injustice of the proceedings leaves him queasy, yet he is hesitant to express himself, fearing that he too will be caught up in the torture machine. When at last his honor is at stake he disapproves frankly. By means of the device of the outsider Kafka gains the anthropological perspective necessary for a penetrating and critical insight into his society.

A tour de force, 'In the Penal Colony' possesses the usual virtues and defects of its genre. Although brilliantly done, it lacks emotional and spiritual complexity. It is full of mordant irony. The condemned man is by no means portrayed as morally superior to the officer. Doglike, he is sadistic in his interest in the officer's execution. Both he and his guard are morally tainted and for this reason the explorer refuses to permit them to accompany him when he leaves the island. The style is extremely vivid. Again the symbol two is prominent.

In its slimness, its anecdotal and confessional quality, and its unique tone, *The Country Doctor* is similar to *Contemplation*. But certain aspects of its fourteen sketches indicate that its author had come far in six years. Style had matured, tone deepened, impressionism had given way to undisputed expressionism. Tenderness had been supplanted by an objective mood of despair. It was as if the author had turned caustically on his softer self in an effort to expunge it. Violence and terror were the new themes. The psyche turned inward and festered. The transmutation of autobiography was more fixed, the sources of inspiration more distant from the results. The author now refused to accept his pain merely as such; he forced it to labor for him, to construct new forms by devising dream-images of itself. Thereby he found release and atonement and a measure of survival.

The masterpiece of the collection is the title story. Its exploitation of the absurd is masterly. It may well be a transcript of a dream touched up by Kafka. Kafka dreamed prolifically, brilliantly. The story appeals to one's night-self. The breathless style and wild invention produce a great effect. The volume is studded with dreamlike sketches—such as 'A Dream' and 'The Law,' both fragments of *The Trial*, and 'Worries of a Family Man.' 'On the Gallery' might have been included in *Contemplation*. A small anecdotal sketch, it seems to point up the loneliness and misery of its author. The young spectator is an outcast; he wishes the circus rider were one too. But life (in the form of the rider) is beautiful, healthy, unselfconscious, and the young man knows it is beyond his reach. He weeps.

'Worries of a Family Man' concerns itself with a thing called Odradek. This too symbolizes life—crazy, silly life, yet immortal and elusive. The narrator cannot grasp it; it makes him think painfully of his own mortality. 'An Old Page' is a poetic imagistic portrayal of disorder and barbarism in a world lacking in faith and brotherhood. It purports to be about the distant, feudal past but is, of course, about the present. 'Fratricide' is a blood-curdling description of murder. Its symbolic meaning is plain: in this world there is no brotherhood and man murders man literally and spiritually, out of sheer lust of killing. Again and again Kafka projects his inner violence outwardly to create prose miniatures of despair: the age is out of joint, he says in 'The New Barrister'; terror stalks the modern world, he says in 'Jackals and Arabs.' The latter must have appealed to him because of its theme of incommensurability. It is in the cards, says Kafka sardonically, for jackals to hate Arabs, for Arabs to oppress and love jackals, and for blood to flow between them. Kafka is hinting at the incommensurability between nature and spirit. 'A Report to an Academy,' the volume's longest piece, aside from its bright satirical tone and its empathy for the ape, is merely an exercise, whose function is to satirize the spiritual in man. The education of the ape, his transformation into a human being, depends upon a system of repression and destruction of memories. Kafka, like Swift, implies that man is a beast.

The style and tone of *The Hunger-Artist*, a booklet of eighty-six pages, put together at Brod's request shortly before Kafka's death, are emphatically different from *Contemplation* and *The Country Doctor*. The tenderness of *Contemplation* and the savagery of *The Country Doctor* are absent; in their stead are calmness and irony. Kafka has simmered down, become didactic. His sudden and burning visions have given way to sustained virtuosity. He now represses not only tenderness but violence as well. He seeks refuge in the aloofness and virtuosity of the artist, simultaneously satirizing him. In effect he ridicules himself, the inhuman self which has survived the double repression and has the audacity of double egotism to sustain it, that very egotism of excessive modesty and secretiveness sometimes verging on sainthood.

Three stories are concerned with the artist type: 'The Hunger-Artist,' 'First Sorrow,' and 'Josephine the Songstress.' The first of these is one of Kafka's best-known tales. It reminds one of the food shortages in Europe during and after the First World War and of the marathon craze that swept the Continent and the United States in the early post-war period. The self-destructiveness of the artist in his attempts to reach great heights of endurance and performance, to set unbelievable records, to endure and achieve the impossible, are themes woven into the story. Another motif is the hunger strike as a political weapon. The artist is viewed as an outcast. He is ridiculous, the slave of a peculiar logic and consistency, all related to the demands of his ego. Inevitably he exploits spirit until spirit injures body. Kafka sympathizes. Unlike the early pieces, 'The Hunger-Artist' has a powerful narrative rhythm, impressive in classic strength and sweep. The style is realistic within the framework of an expressionistic *leitmotif*. Perhaps most impressive are Kafka's empathetic, imaginative talents.

In 'Josephine the Songstress,' a story of about seven thousand words, Kafka studies the artist for the last time. According to Brod, 'Josephine' is Kafka's final work. The tale moves powerfully although somewhat didactically. It is told as though in one breath, as if by sheer naive inspiration. Now the artist, seen from the point of view of the audience, is presented as an enigma. The implications of spiritual arrogance, of spirit as egotism and egotism as spirit, are obvious. Music as the choice of Josephine's art is a bit of irony directed at the author. There is also irony in the fact that the audience is incapable of detecting any music in Josephine's singing. It accepts her because of her immense self-confidence, which it transfers to itself. A masochistic touch is Kafka's choice of a mouse to represent the artist. Besides being an artistic mouse, Josephine is also something of a mountebank. Again the theme of incommensurability is displayed—in this case between the artist and his audience.

'First Sorrow,' the short piece about a trapeze artist, exploits the ridiculousness of the extremist as well as his sadness in solitude. The tale, in fable form, portrays the artist's childishness. The artist is motivated by his desire for perfection, which later becomes 'habit grown tyrannical,' something that Kafka discusses from personal experience. 'A Little Woman' is a minor sketch, not so much a narrative as a talking around the subject. Its motifs are introversion, despair, fear, loneliness, acute self-analysis, sick scrupulosity.

The Great Wall of China, published posthumously, contains some of Kafka's most interesting short fiction. Undoubtedly much of it was composed before *The Hunger-Artist*. We treat it at this point only in order to adhere to publishing chronology, since there is no other dependable record. One of its finest and most revealing tales is 'The Married Couple,' a story of the powers of woman as contrasted with the sickliness of man. Kafka views women as full of spiritual and mental health and power, especially within the framework of marriage. Men are diseased, racked by ambition and intellect. The narrator murders old N. by inducing a stroke in him with his compulsive talk. The three men react helplessly, cowering before the old man's death. Then the wife enters with the nightshirt she has warmed before the fire for her husband, and wakes him. She defeats death by her inability to recognize it.

Many of the stories are exceedingly brief. 'The Silence of the Sirens' is a not very meaningful oddity in which Kafka splits a few hairs about the Ulysses myth and the sirens. 'Prometheus' is but a comment on the legend. 'Sancho Panza' is one of Kafka's tiny parables that delight in turning accepted

[83]

legends inside out. 'A Common Confusion,' a fable of the disconnectedness of things earthly and human, is a comedy of errors, interesting because of its use of letters to represent people and places. 'The Problem of Our Laws' is a statement in parable form of the confusion attendant on the supremacy of cabalas—in this instance cabalas nurtured by the nobility. It is, among other things, a representation of the struggle between an outmoded classicism and a youthful romanticism. It indicates Kafka's profound interest in the social sphere.

'The Bucket Rider' and 'The Hunter Gracchus' are superb tales. The first is a fantasy which concerns the freezing of a man who is out of coal and has no money to buy any. His stove 'breathes out cold.' The narrator hopes to persuade the coal dealer, on grounds of humanity, to credit him with just a bit more coal. He gets into his coal bucket and it transports him over the streets to the dealer's. But the dealer's wife pretends not to notice him. Kafka sees man here as possessing a conscience and woman as being cold and selfish. In 'The Hunter Gracchus' a hunter has been killed in an accident, yet he has not entered the next world. He is constantly roving the earth in an effort to leave it, to be done with life and to enter the true and unequivocal death. Kafka implies sardonically that there is an incommensurability between death and the hereafter, just as between man and man. The states of incompletion, of wandering, of suspension and despair, need not be limited to this life but may also exist in death. Death is therefore by no means the release it is commonly thought to be. Thus even in death there are outcasts. But poor Gracchus is an outcast from the living as well. The tale is more conventional in form than most of Kafka's small efforts. It contains a setting in the beginning, the projection of atmosphere, and is more rounded. It is witty rather than gruesome. This supernatural projection of the Sisyphus theme is thick with Kafka's personal symbols—the number two, the color yellow, candle, et cetera.

Kafka's novellas generally excel in invention and imaginative fantasy. Their defect is their too-close adherence to allegory, at the expense of symbolism. An exception is 'Investigations of a Dog,' which we have already discussed. One of the least rewarding of the novellas is 'The Burrow,' which is obsessive in tone and almost entirely humorless. It dramatizes an anxiety neurosis. The fear mechanism, out of control, dominates the organism even when there is no immediate danger. The novella exemplifies intellectual fabrication rather than imaginative ferment. Its superabundance of tireless and tiresome invention is depressing. This inclination to prolixity and sheer virtuosity is typical of Kafka's final period.

'The Giant Mole' was written as early as 1914. 'The Great Wall of China' is of somewhat later vintage. Unfortunately both, like 'The Burrow,' are fragmentary. 'The Giant Mole' is interesting because of its satire on scientific authorities—not, as Muir asserts, on the authority of science. 'The Great Wall of China' implies the incommensurability between evidence and knowledge, the disorder of life and the confusion of time and space. It often seems an unconscious dramatization of the principle of equivalence in the theory of relativity. The incomplete 'Blumfeld, An Elderly Bachelor,' published posthumously, is a delightful creation whose time of composition is obscure. It is a sketch of loneliness and bachelorhood, in which the inanimate seems human and the human seems mechanical. Blumfeld carries his bachelor's commonsense to fantastic limits. He does not run out to the street to call for witnesses to the miracle of the two bouncing balls. On the contrary, he hides the miracle as if it were a sign of his secret guilt. And indeed it is: of his guilt of difference. The balls chose Blumfeld as the object of their parasitism because of his eccentricity. Blumfeld knows this; that is why he hides them from the landlady.

A number of small items were all published posthumously —'The Denial,' 'The Departure,' 'At Night,' 'The Helmsman,' 'The Examination,' 'Advocates,' 'Return,' 'Community.' They appeared first in volume five of the six-volume collected German edition. Some of them are reminiscent of *Contemplation*. 'The Denial' reminds one of 'The Great Wall of China'; 'Advocates,' of *The Trial*. All have the usual insistence on paradox and self-cancellation. Other posthumous pieces, appearing in volume six of the collected edition, are 'The Thorn Thicket,' 'In Our Synagogue,' 'The Appeal,' 'A Guest Among the Dead,' 'New Lamps,' and 'The Sword.' The last three of these seem to be dreams Kafka jotted down. 'A Guest Among the Dead' and 'In Our Synagogue' are interesting mainly because Kafka mentions Jews and Jewish religious symbols. Kafka rarely speaks of Jews or Judaism in his fiction. Generally he uses religious symbols drawn from Christianity—as if he wishes to forget he is a member of a minority group.

The Novels

KAFKA's tragic heroes reflect their author in innumerable ways, among them increasing age and mellowness. As the impact of his failure to marry recedes, the significance of the father slowly abates. Kafka's progressive disease acted as a comfort and a shock absorber.

The youngest hero, Karl Rossmann, is naively neurotic; his older brother, Joseph K., is savagely neurotic; K. is philosophically neurotic. Karl was conceived in 1912, during Kafka's first struggles with himself during his affair with F.B. He is a personal hero. Joseph K. was conceived in 1914, just before the outbreak of the war, when Kafka's relations with F.B., like those between the nations, were at a critical point. He is less personal than Karl and assumes complex social overtones. His savagery is as representative of the state of world affairs as of his creator's masochistic torments. K. was conceived around 1922. The war was over and Bohemia liberated from the Austrian tyranny. Kafka was beset by a malignant disease. Yet his personal problems were not so acute as ten years earlier. K. reflects these factors.

Karl Rossmann's problem is sexual. He strives to achieve heterosexual stability. This was the problem of his creator in 1912. Joseph K.'s is that of bachelorhood, with its loneliness, freedom, daemonism. He reflects Kafka's notions at a time when marriage, even with F.B., seemed to him a violation of his sanctity. For K. a heterosexual arrangement is not only necessary but feasible and he achieves one with Frieda. Shortly after writing *The Castle*, Kafka began to live with Dora Dymant.

These three heroes, who are not heroic in the romantic sense, are the dangling young men of the modern novel. Their world is thin, with little furniture, most of it rotten. They are bewildered by the authority of specialization and the crushing burden of accumulated facts. They resent the interim period in which they live and the remoteness of their fathers' world. They resent the collapse of faith visible all around them. They are unwilling to sublimate their personal neurosis in the collective neurosis of a shallow faith. Therefore they forge a profound neurosis of their own. They refuse to believe in the baseless simply because it is an anchor. On the other hand, they cannot find faith in disbelief. Therefore they dangle. They are not men of action. They possess no stage and their muscles are cramped, their bones mildewed. Worst of all, they lack the heart for action. Nor are they men of experience. Being deprived of myths, they are overwhelmed by the complexity and irrationality of nature; therefore they turn their backs on her, avert their eyes before beauty, shun truth as a plague except when verbalizing it, dangling it with themselves. They are more interested in arguing 'What is truth?' than examining some of its causes and effects. They are thin abstractions of men, dangling in universal space, obsessed by memories of the womb, yet too modern, too faithless to crawl back to its warmth through the medium of shallow and decaying religions.

Amerika is Kafka's pre-war effort, his trial flight, his finger exercise in the field of the novel. His artistic breakthrough, which was one of the consequences of his meeting with F.B., permitted as well as necessitated more sustained work than his hitherto fragmentary efforts, many of them merely diary selections. The narrative element flourished as invention grew abundant and conceptions streamed in. 'The Verdict' gave way to the first chapter of *Amerika*, 'The Stoker.' This gave way to *The Metamorphosis*, and this in turn to *Amerika*, the full-length novel. One may inquire whether the novel form was suited to Kafka's thematic and artistic needs, since he completed no novels, while finishing several works in the intermediate form. It seems probable that the extensive requirements of the novel were exorbitant in the face of work so highly cathartic as Kafka's. Themes resulted from immediate personal situations and needs that required immediate outlets. But often these needs lessened before the work was done; the cathartic and therapeutic values evaporated, new themes and inspirations replaced the old, and finishing was more a matter of discipline than catharsis. Professional discipline Kafka, the persistent amateur, abhorred.

'The Verdict' and *The Metamorphosis* were autobiographical projections, imaginative prostrations of the son before the father. *Amerika*, on the other hand, was an escape from the father, also an escape from the sterile Europe of 1912 and from personal problems such as the relationship with F.B. America is the classic land of escape—from European persecutions, unhappy family life, from the economic and moral poverty of the Old World. Kafka viewed it as such, as the almost unspoiled land, the only slightly questionable utopia. Nevertheless the escape occurred only on the most superficial levels, in terms of environment and plot. Underneath these, in the strata of a cabalistic web of symbols, the real world intruded and in the last analysis dominated the brilliant upper world, distorting its face. The father played a more subtle but more pervading role than in 'The Verdict' and *The Metamorphosis*. The fiancée played it partly through a series of fictional women—Clara, Therese, Brunelda—but mainly through the theme, the importance of heterosexuality, domesticity as personal salvation. Europe played it through the emphasis on bureaucracy and through the closed-in air of the book that was to deal with open spaces. *Amerika* is the first-born of three major siblings. It is cruder than the others, more graphic, less chiaroscuro. Its humor is more broad, its conceptions more personal and narrow, its style less subtle, more dilute, its expressionism closer to burlesque than to dreams.

The Trial is the strongest product of Kafka's father period, a novel of bachelorhood, the city, masochism. Its sadism, uniforms, stalking terror, mass obedience, drumhead courts are representative of the era of expanding, exploding militarism. It is Kafka's first major attempt to deal with the social sphere of his theme. *The Trial* is by no means a surface escape from the father; on the contrary it is a direct challenge and accusation of him, a fictional precursor to the *Letter to My Father*. Nor is it an escape from Kafka's Europe; it is rather a savage indictment of it. In a sense it is the atonement for the effort to run away in *Amerika*. This explains the self-flagellation, the hysteria, the destruction of the hero, who no longer represents the author in the escapist guise of youth, as a sixteen-year-old, but is exactly the same age as himself. The style is violent, the dream technique achieves a climax, the humor is most sardonic. The father appears as in a nightmare, intent on destroying the son, an Abraham with the sacrificial knife in hand. Isaac, the son, once having seen the knife, forever longs for it. Lacking the faith of the father and identifying Abraham with Jehovah, he is convinced of his guilt and demands its expiation. Birth, life, and death are seen in terms of a trial, with the end foreordained. It is a novel of monstrous visions, a personal vindication of the author as well as his indictment and destruction. The father is now seen as the group-father, the philistine, the man of night, of tenements, sewers, prejudice, superstition. *The Trial* is sex in stasis, sex recoiling on itself; it is sexual terror and inability to compromise, to share oneself.

Kafka, the artist of despair, fattened off his personal misfortunes. In two short, passionate years his style became plastic and visionary, his symbolism more subterranean than ever, although carrying greater social implications. His myth-making power grew astoundingly, his dialectical skill found epic release. His conceptions became integrated and indigenous. They mirrored the signs of the dying faith, of a society in its death rattle. Kafka achieved this by a juggling of symbols, a complex of metaphors. He had neither time nor patience for documentation. He placed his final faith, the remnants of it, in the seemingly indestructible, in the poetic, the visionary, this being the extent of his religiousness.

The Castle, product of Kafka's maturity, is 'old age,' a backward glance out of the comfort of disease at the tumultuous times of struggle for salvation through heterosexuality. At the same time it is a foreshadowing, in its abundance of domestic and fertility symbols, of the joyous heterosexual phase which was to follow. Its landscape is modeled on the landscape of Zürau. If 1917 marked the end of his relations with F.B., it did not end his preoccupation with the related problems of father, marriage, and domesticity. The highly personal tone of *Amerika* and the savage self-immolation tone of *The Trial* are gone. The nightmare element is subdued, the expressionistic effects are restrained. Life is no longer all garbage and sewers. The air is more open, wafted by the breath of the countryside. The father is no longer Abraham with the knife. If he is Abraham at all he is an Abraham bored with his Isaac, finding him unworthy of the sacrifice. It is Isaac who tries to lead Abraham to the mountain, stalking him in pursuit of his own self-sacrifice. The drama is less acute, for there is no knife, no lifting of the faithful, sacrificial hand. *The Castle* is a post-war product. The murdering and shrieking are over. There is a ghastly stillness in the land. Men have returned to the soil for strength. The battle of the cities is ended.

The Castle is a study of the dilemma of marriage. The two horns on which Kafka impaled himself and which he sometimes describes in his diaries—independence and irresponsibility on the one hand, necessity to compromise and to account for one's actions on the other—are symbolized by the castle and the village. The castle is bachelorhood (all the gentry are unmarried). It is uncompromising, irresponsible. It is solitude, freedom of motion. It is also, however, sterility, silliness, old-maidish fussiness, remoteness from the basic concerns of life. The village is domesticity, fertility, compromise, responsibility, abbreviation of personal freedom. But it is also gossip, maliciousness, stolidity, mental blindness. K. wants both—both the impossible refinement of the one and the domestic oblivion of the other. Having won Frieda, he loses her by his attraction to the castle. *The Castle* is also a comment on feudalism. Done on feudal ground, in the country, when feudalism was finally wiped out with the collapse of the Empire, it is a description in perspective of the gigantic cabala which had sat on Bohemia's head since 1620. It was Kafka's genius to be able to find symbols that could carry the weight of simultaneous levels, beginning with the autobiographical and sinking ever deeper in the subterranean world of cabalistic social structures and the personal and collective unconscious.

Expressionism is a nose-thumbing attack on realism and naturalism in the arts. It refuses to lumber along with their baggage. Kafka, however, was unusually mild in his revolt. He was mainly interested in content and effect rather than in the various tactical revolutions that kept the German expressionist school alive for its time. He is a stylistic eclectic. His quarrel was only with the substance of the older art forms.

The nightmare motif is a favorite in his mad world. Social relations are presented in a fantastic manner: people break all the rules, they are either too familiar or too shy. Conventional notions of time and space are rudely violated. We are never sure that a wall is in place or that a door has not walked away. Kafka's people are always misjudging distance, speaking too loudly in a small room and too softly in a large one. His world is fluid; and the chief fluid is emotions. Characters swim in emotions, and time and space are dependent on them. Walls recede before an angry man and close in on a timid one. Mind exists only as a subordinate, perspectival, and dissonant form of emotion. This is romanticism carried to its extreme. Kafka is the last frontier between reason and chaos. Beyond him there is only meaningless babble. His exaggeration is effective. It is the primitive, the uninhibited, the unrestrained on display. It is an excellent cathartic. It throws into sudden relief things normally hidden because taken for granted. His characters are possessed. They have a way of concentrating ferociously on irrelevant details precisely when they are preoccupied with important matters. This is one of Kafka's techniques for creating ambivalence in the reader while demonstrating it in his people.

Kafka's main effects are dependent on his intermingling of realism and distortion. It is this which gives his work its dream quality. In *Amerika* the mixture is not as homogeneous as in the later novels. There are stretches of realism more or less unalleviated by expressionism. One such barren section occurs in the captain's cabin, in a description of waterfront activity. This is mild compared to the pages in Chapter II dealing with Karl's education. Kafka without his dream-distortion is disappointing. Once having become accustomed to the unexpected, we despise the easily guessed. Kafka is often derivative in his first novel, still dependent on such realistic masters as Dickens. In theme, however, he is original and mature.

One of the important thematic motifs in *Amerika* is that the hero is blameless, that his fate is cloudy, and that he is abnormally susceptible to feelings of guilt. Kafka's protagonists are innocents among the worldly, yet they suffer guilt more intensely than the sinners. Another important motif is the idea of trial, which recurs in *Amerika* with ever-intensified variations. The first trial is that of the stoker before the captain. It is a typically Kafkian trial, in that the defendant insists on being tried, loses himself in a morass of sophistry and irrationality before reaching even a long-range view of justice, and wrestles with a sense of guilt of which he is unaware and which is the ultimate cause of his downfall. The stoker's trial differs from the usual pattern only in that the defendant is illogical and incoherent, while Karl, K., and Joseph K. are the essence of logic and reason; that is, it is not one of the protagonists who is on trial.

If the case of the stoker is a miniature *Trial,* it is also a miniature *Castle.* The castle is the captain's cabin. The captain is the count, his officers the high-class bureaucrats; he suavely says almost nothing, maintaining the silence and isolation and incomprehensibility proper to the castle. The interesting difference is that now we are inside the castle. Because of Karl's good luck in coming upon Uncle Jacob and because of his ready identification with the masters in the room, we view the trial from above, from the perspective of the castle inhabitants. Gently and somewhat condescendingly Karl asks the stoker: 'Why don't you say something? Why do you put up with everything?' This is the basic anti-cabalistic question, which Kafka never uses in the more mature novels, since it is too transparent for his theme. Later he avoids transparencies in order that the reader's identification with the protagonist may be complete and the catharsis effective.

Wealth and poverty are handled as motifs in *Amerika*—a challenge to those critics who assert Kafka was without a social conscience. Karl defends a simple laboring man, is accepted by the wealthy, politically powerful bourgeoisie in the form of Uncle Jacob, and is kind to the stoker. Later, after undergoing his uncle's ministrations, he allies himself with the luxury class. On the way to Pollunder's he sees a demonstration of metal workers; but he merely leans back happily on the arm of Pollunder. '. . . the knowledge that he would soon be a welcome guest in a well-lighted country house surrounded by high walls and guarded by watch-dogs filled him with extravagant well-being . . .'

A second trial is that of Karl before Pollunder and Green. Again all the familiar details of Kafka's trials are present. Karl wishes so intensely to leave Pollunder's house that he overstates his case and places himself in a position to be judged by the two men. 'And once he had put the worst into words, all the rest came pouring out after it, and he said without the slightest insincerity things of which he had never even thought before.' His long speech is typical of the weak introvert pleading before the extrovert who is impressed only by personality and power. Karl is like a Gulliver among coarse giants who speak a strange tongue and treat him contemptuously. He is a pygmy of an ego beside the two vulgarians. Once he has finished speaking he realizes that he has condemned himself and that both men are now his judges. This is made clear by the shifting of Pollunder in Karl's psychological spectrum. 'Mr. Pollunder's kindness and Mr. Green's loathesomeness ran into a blur together, and all that he asked from that smoky room was permission to leave. He felt cut off from Mr. Pollunder, prepared to do battle against Mr. Green, and yet all round him was a vague fear, whose impact troubled his sight.' This second trial is more complete than the first, since this time sentence is passed. 'Before you go,' says Green, 'you must say good-bye to Miss Clara.' 'Yes,' says Pollunder, 'you must do that.' To say good-bye to Miss Clara is to overstay his leave and to doom himself. The walk down the corridor to Miss Clara's room with the jailer-servant is like the last few steps to the execution chamber.

A third trial, before the headwaiter of the Hotel Occidental, proceeds on the lines of the first two with the difference that now the bureaucratic element is emphasized.

Two lines of symbolism may be traced in *Amerika*, both unique, yet interweaving and impinging on each other. The first of these relates to the problem of authority, the second to the sex education of Karl Rossmann. For Kafka there is no clear emotional distinction between parental authority and authority in general. For him authority is essentially male. Woman is a kind of Greek chorus of comfort who is somehow present. In *Amerika* the protagonist reacts sexually to male authority. He tends to develop 'crushes' on males who are unattached and to immerse himself in them in the way in which woman is conventionally supposed to lose herself in man.

The nameless stoker is inconsistent and irrational, a complete egotist, like the rest of Karl's opponents. But Karl is attracted to him. 'Lie down on the bunk, you'll have more room there,' says the man. An impossible suggestion from a stranger, in the circumstances. Yet, what is even more impossible, Karl accepts. Not only that, he enjoys it: 'Karl scrambled in as well as he could, and laughed aloud at his first unsuccessful attempt to swing himself over.' This is quite a sudden change from the strained relations in the preceding paragraph, where the man roars at Karl for hammering on the door. Karl is attracted by chaos and violence. When he tries to be rational, saying he must go up to the deck to see about his luggage, the stoker treats him abominably, 'giving him a push with one hand on the chest, quite roughly, so that he fell back on the bunk again.' Karl is momentarily exasperated. Then, when the stoker announces his profession, Karl cries out with delight. The suggestion of masochism is obvious. Karl tries to act independently and is manhandled; he responds with admiration. In the captain's cabin he is stoked into launching a defense of his companion. Like a furnace he can be inflamed. In the role of the stoker's advocate he is the ego rampant, full of self-confidence and euphoria. He is talented as an object to be stoked. He is a neurotic and a pariah and therefore susceptible. The stoker is for him a father image, a symbol of the father as brute strength, irrationality, and inarticulateness. Karl's affection for him verges on the sexual. He strokes his fingers, kisses his hand, and altogether seems unnaturally fond of him.

The stoker gives way artistically before the second father image, Uncle Jacob, shifting from a figure of size and importance to an insignificant figure whose destiny concerns no one. In the meantime the inconspicuous man with the bamboo cane slowly emerges into the foreground until, in a close-up, we see the second surrogate to be presented. Uncle Jacob, like the stoker, is a man of size. He symbolizes the burgher, money, social standing, the father as solid citizen. His letter of excommunication to Karl in Chapter III could have been written by Theobald Pontifex in *The Way of All Flesh*. He stokes Karl in the life of wealth. Like the high-powered bourgeois that he is, he tolerates no idleness or bohemianism. At first he is straightforward with his nephew; then suddenly, in a meeting with Pollunder and Green, he assumes all the usual parental irrationality. In Chapter II there is no sexual overtone in Karl's attitude toward his uncle, but in the following chapter we find it clearly. Karl, thinking how good it will be to get away from Pollunder and return to his uncle, daydreams of rushing happily into his uncle's bedroom in the morning, although he does not even know where the bedroom is. He will surprise his uncle, 'whom until now he had known only full dressed and buttoned to the chin, sitting up in bed in his night-shirt. . .' And at dinner Green emphasizes Uncle Jacob's solicitousness over Karl: '. . . his affection for Karl was too great to be called the mere affection of an uncle.'

In Chapter III Pullunder assumes the father-image role. Although he was extremely pleasant in the presence of Uncle Jacob, once he reaches his own house he is suddenly presumptuous and condescending toward Karl. To Clara, his daughter, he says: 'He is only Jacob's nephew, his own name is Karl Rossmann.' In a moment he is full of the irritability of authority when he cries 'Impossible!' on hearing that Green will be present that evening. ' "Why should he come just this evening?" said Pollunder, and the words rolled furiously over his sagging lower lip, which like all loose, heavy flesh was easily agitated.' Karl is stoked: ' "Perhaps he'll soon go away again," remarked Karl, himself astonished at the sympathy uniting him to these people who had been complete strangers to him a day ago.' Now Green assumes the father-image role while Pollunder recedes into the background. Pollunder is the rotarian, Green the vulgarian. Karl suffers a violent aversion to Green and can barely eat his dinner. Green is a sensualist and this dismays the squeamish, fragile Karl. The latter cannot understand how Pollunder's attitude toward Green has abruptly changed at the table. He has not grasped the fact that Pollunder is of a kind with Green and that he, Karl, is the sole introvert, the sole pariah, in the room.

All these father images—the stoker, Uncle Jacob, Pollunder, and Green—are men without mates. Even Pollunder, the father of Clara, is never mentioned in connection with a wife. It is because they are mateless that they are accessible to Karl's crushes. This accessibility is a necessary ingredient of Kafka's figures of authority in *Amerika*. Karl can be dominated and hypnotized by men. With women it is different—he will resist them firmly and even violently, as we see in his tussle with Clara. Men elicit into the open all his neurotic traits. He permits them to dominate and befuddle him. Women can mother or seduce him, even use physical force on him, without his losing his aggressiveness. He is safer with them than with men because with them he is not ambivalent. He does not know this—or does not wish to know it. In general he is cool to Pollunder and Green, for they form a pair against him, which makes each remote from him.

We have now completed an examination of the first three chapters. These form a unit distinct from any other in the novel. They deal with a succession of father images all of which oppress the protagonist. From them he learns the meaning of personal, capricious, and arbitrary authority.

Chapter IV, 'The Road to Rameses,' is the story of Karl's experience in meeting and joining up with two job-seekers, Delamarche and Robinson. Here again the motif of the pair enters the symbolic tissue. The two men are extroverts, practical men of the working class, shrewd and hard-bitten. They are inaccessible to Karl's advances, therefore they do not represent authority for him and he is not ambivalent toward them. He resists them as readily as he resisted Clara. For all their hostility toward him, the four father images did not commit definite ethical breaches against him. They tyrannized him subtly, in the way of authority, and he was helpless, being under the homosexual spell. But toward Delamarche and Robinson he is platonic, therefore he can exact justice from them. Although he permits them to exploit him mercilessly, when they commit acts which are obviously unethical he knows how to be outspoken and determined. If the platonic element is dominant in this chapter, nevertheless the father image and the crush are not altogether absent. The loss of the photo frees Karl from his father's domination, setting him upon the platonic stage of his sexual progress. It also revenges him against his parents (its loss is a symbolic murder of them) because they exiled him to America. The stealing and supposed destruction of the photograph are unexplained—they are purely symbolic. That Karl unconsciously wanted to lose the photograph is indicated by his exaggerated show of righteousness against the offenders.

In Chapter v, 'The Hotel Occidental,' Karl, having broken with Delamarche and Robinson, free of disturbing father images and the photograph of his parents, is eminently successful in his external relations with people. He is efficient as an elevator boy and 'the brasswork in his lift was the most brightly polished of all. . .' He is no longer the blunderer who lost an umbrella and a luggage box and who could not find his way about Pollunder's home. Moreover, he succeeds with women, the manageress and Therese—but on a platonic basis only. In his trips with Therese to Rameses he is actually an extrovert in his efficiency and self-confidence. He seems to have lost his neurosis.

The most striking development in Chapter vi is that Robinson is now alone; Delamarche does not appear throughout the long chapter. Robinson is therefore accessible to Karl and to the old neurotic ambivalence. Robinson 'looks quite different,' in Karl's words. He begins making physical overtures and we realize that the homosexual motif is in full swing again. ' "Wouldn't you like to come and see us, Rossmann. We're living in great style now," said Robinson, leering seductively at Karl.' Karl asks whether the invitation comes from Robinson or Delamarche. When Robinson replies that it comes from both, Karl rejects the invitation, realizing that he would still be excluded by the pair. Robinson proceeds to make a nuisance of himself and to involve Karl with the hotel authorities. But the basic cause of Karl's difficulties is his inability to act efficiently in ridding himself of Robinson. Instead of calling the guards and having Robinson ejected, Karl tries to hide him and thereby neglects his lift. This obsessive desire to hide him, as if he were the skeleton in his closet, is a tacit admission that he wishes to keep him.

Karl's lift partner, Rennell, is with Delamarche, a hint that he has replaced Robinson in Delamarche's favor, thus forming a new pair and making Robinson eligible as an object for Karl's crushes. Karl's sexual ambivalence is symbolized in a sentence: 'So Karl managed to guide Robinson, who had now become somewhat used to walking, as far as Rennell's bed without rousing much attention, for the bed was quite near the door and luckily unoccupied; in his own bed, as he could see from the distance, a strange boy whom he did not know was quietly sleeping.' Karl deposits Robinson in Rennell's bed instead of his own, thus making Rennell liable to punishment for harboring a stranger in the dormitory. This is his revenge on Rennell for freeing Robinson from his relationship with Delamarche, thus exposing him, Karl, to danger. The homosexual element is heightened by the fact that a strange boy is sleeping in Karl's bed, an exteriorization of Karl's hidden desire. From this point on Karl is doomed. What aids his ruin is his insistence on defending himself with absolute logic and unadulterated truth.

The first six chapters of *Amerika* consist of two segments of three chapters each, the first portraying the narcissistic or homosexual factor in Karl's education, the second the platonic in terms of both male and female. The second segment concludes with the temptation and fall of Karl. Since the first two units of Kafka's plan consist of three chapters each, it would be a fair supposition to assume that the third would also contain three chapters. The German edition of the collected works contains only two, plus two fragments. The English translation contains the two chapters without the fragments. The two Brunelda fragments, which precede the final chapter, were probably meant to constitute the major part of an unfinished chapter, Chapter VIII.

That the third unit deals with the heterosexual factor in Karl's education is made clear almost at once by the fact that Rennell has suddenly dropped out of the picture, leaving Delamarche alone with Brunelda in a sordid 'affair' in which he is being kept by her. Brunelda is undoubtedly the most unpleasant woman in all Kafka, yet she manages to convey the notion of healthy female fertility, which is also suggested by the prominent motif of children. Children are everywhere, mostly underfoot.

Just before entering Brunelda's apartment for the first time Karl sees three women in the corridor. 'Don't look this way,' Delamarche snaps at Karl. But Karl shakes his head angrily, refusing to accept admonitions from Delamarche. '. . . he had just begun walking towards the women, to make his meaning clear, when Robinson caught him by the sleeve. . .' This is the first instance of Karl's sexual aggressiveness toward women. Robinson aids the heterosexual theme by his constant and suggestive references to Brunelda's desirability. He says, for example, 'Then she lifted up her skirt and wiped my eyes with the hem. Who knows what more she might have done if Delamarche hadn't called her and she hadn't had to go back into the room again at once. I thought, of course, that it was my turn next, and I asked through the curtain if I couldn't come in.' A variation of the theme is the love-making of couples. 'At some of the windows could be seen loving couples standing quite motionless; one of these couples was standing at a window opposite; the young man had his arm round the girl and was squeezing her waist.' Karl himself does not indulge in heterosexual relations; he is only exposed to them as an observer. Brunelda is a Brünnehilde type, the lusty, powerful female. Karl Rossmann recalls the fate of Siegmund in *The Valkyrie*, who says: '. . . whate'er I did, where'er I fared, if friend I sought or woman wooed, still was I held in suspicion. Ill fate lay on me. Whate'er to me seemed right, others reckoned it ill; whate'er I held to be foul, others counted as fair. In feuds I fell where'er I dwelt, wrath ever against me I roused; sought I for gladness, found I but grief; so must I "Woeful" call me, for woe still walks in my wake.' Siegmund's woe, like Karl's, resulted from the loss of his father.

The two Brunelda fragments are the most inspired writing in *Amerika*. The wealth of invention, the height which the expressionist technique attains, the bustling irony, satire, and humor, the pathos found here combine to present a brilliant surface beneath which one feels the presence of a complex and dramatic symbolism. The first fragment follows in narrative time immediately upon the close of Chapter VII. It opens with Karl's awaking in the morning and portrays the bathing of Brunelda by Delamarche and the fetching of breakfast by Robinson and Karl. Karl catches glimpses of Brunelda's nude neck, she waves her undergarments in the air to lure Robinson beyond the partition to rescue her from Delamarche's awkward washing, she threatens to jump out of the tub and run around as she is. A wonderful scene follows in which Karl and Robinson search vainly for Brunelda's perfume. A striking change is evident in Karl in this fragment. He is very solicitous about the appearance of the breakfast and actually takes the tray out of Robinson's hands because it doesn't seem safe enough with him. He is even obsequious before Brunelda. 'Next time I'll do better,' he says, after Brunelda and Delamarche have already expressed their satisfaction. Only the evening before he was determined to escape from the menage. Incomplete as the fragment is, one senses that Karl is accepting his fate with Brunelda and making the best of it.

The second fragment is the story of Brunelda's moving out of her room. Delamarche and Robinson are neither present nor mentioned. The impression is that Karl has supplanted them. Now we see him as very capable. With the aid of the student he manages to get Brunelda downstairs in her invalid's chair and wheels her off. She is no longer the self-willed Brünnehilde of *The Valkyrie;* now she has met her master, as in *The Twilight of the Gods.* She is meek and mortified and helpless, completely in Karl's power. She is so daunted by her misery and helplessness that she covers herself with a large gray cloth as they make their way through the streets. A policeman stops them to investigate. Karl handles him masterfully. Then a man wheeling milk cans attaches himself to them and makes sly attempts to discover what is beneath the cloth. Karl is protective, even gentle and loving; he behaves as though he were her lover. They arrive at an establishment. The implication is that they will live there together. Karl is gratified by the good impression she makes on the manager of the place. He has reached the climax of the heterosexual phase.

The symbolism of the Oklahoma chapter is clear: Karl at last finds a niche for himself, no matter how small. The theme of heterosexuality is brilliantly symbolized. The hundreds of women blowing trumpets are costumed as angels, while the men who relieve them every two hours are dressed as devils—women as the redeeming force, men as the cause of Karl's downfall. Prominent are the couple wheeling a child in a perambulator, the only instance in the novel of a complete representation of heterosexual domesticity.

In the epilogue to the American edition of *The Trial* Brod states: 'For the division into chapters . . . Kafka is responsible, but for the arrangement of the chapters I have had to depend on my own judgment. Since, however, my friend had read me a great part of the manuscript, my judgment has been supported by actual recollection.' One may well question the sequence of chapters in two instances.

Both Chapters IV ('Fräulein Bürstner's Friend') and V ('The Whipper') are unusual because of their brevity. It seems aesthetically strange that they should appear between the two lengthy and powerful chapters, 'In the Empty Interrogation Chamber' and 'K.'s Uncle.' There is no sequence between them, no carry-over of narration or dramatic or psychological tension or development. They burden the first half of the book with an atomistic and jumpy character foreign to Kafka's work. Brod has overlooked a simpler and more artistic arrangement, one more pregnant with meaning. Besides, there is internal evidence that the chapters have been improperly arranged.

In Chapter IV, which follows Joseph K.'s experiences at the slum-court, Frau Grubach says to him: 'You have no idea how I have suffered during these last few days,' referring to his anger at her near the end of Chapter I. The reference to a few days agrees with the time mentioned at the beginning of the chapter: 'In the next few days K. found it impossible to exchange even a word with Fräulein Bürstner.' If Chapter IV is seen as following immediately upon Chapter I, the passage of a few days seems plausible and suitable. Chapter I concludes with K.'s striving for some sort of relationship with Fräulein Bürstner. Then in Chapter IV, in the next few days, he finds it impossible to get hold of her. When he runs into Frau Grubach she is still hurt from his recent anger.

Under the present arrangement, in which Chapter IV is separated from Chapter I by the two large chapters dealing with K.'s visits to the court, this psychological plausibility disappears. The time lapse occurring between Chapters I and IV, amounting to about two weeks, makes Frau Grubach's remark about her suffering 'during these last few days' meaningless, since a good deal more than a few days have passed.

Chapters I and IV are the only two chapters in which Fräulein Bürstner plays a significant role. Setting them adjacent to each other illuminates Joseph K.'s dependence on Fräulein Bürstner; keeping them apart does violence to the significance for him of Fräulein Bürstner and of women in general. At the end of Chapter I K. is desperately seeking allies to counteract his sense of queerness, accentuated by his arrest. After Frau Grubach turns him down (like the inspector she declines his proffered hand), Fräulein Bürstner also rebuffs him—because of his strange behavior. In Chapter IV he continues to woo her and is rebuffed anew, this time not only by Fräulein Bürstner but by Lanz and Fräulein Montag as well.

Chapter IV would precede Chapter II very plausibly because it would motivate K.'s invention in II of a joiner named Lanz—he sees Lanz for the first time close at hand in Chapter IV. K.'s invention is clearly his revenge on the man who together with Fräulein Montag rebuffed him and stood in the way of his getting at Fräulein Bürstner.

As for Chapter V, 'The Whipper,' internally there is evidence that K. has complained to the examining magistrate about the warders: the warders say as much; therefore V must appear subsequent to II. It can follow either II or III or IV. To follow III ('In the Empty Interrogation Chamber') seems fruitless; to follow IV, as at present, seems even more so; but if it follows II, then several effects are created. First, K.'s sudden sadism toward the accused client (in III) is motivated: he is acting now under the influence of the sadism of the whipper chapter. Second, his own amazing hysterical reaction in the empty chamber is motivated by his knowledge of the brutality and efficiency of the court, learned in the whipper chapter. There would thus be an artistic and a psychological progression of mood under the new arrangement which is utterly lacking at present.

The sequence of chapters I propose is the following: 'The Arrest,' 'Fräulein Bürstner's Friend,' 'First Interrogation,' 'The Whipper,' 'In the Empty Interrogation Chamber.'

For the convenience of the reader, however, I shall in general discuss the chapters in the sequence in which they now stand.

Although *The Castle* is generally considered to be Kafka's best novel, many readers prefer *The Trial* for its greater drama and economy, qualities that are in striking evidence when the novel is compared with the loose, picaresque *Amerika. The Trial* is spiritual autobiography of manhood rather than of adolescence as is *Amerika.* It is beautiful in a geometrical sense, in its perfect agreement of style and vision. Its symbolism is a basic part of the vision, as if the vision were experienced symbolically. The dynamics of the novel are the dynamics of the interplay of its symbols. Kafka is a purifying force in the modern novel. He returns to primal effects, making his novel carry meanings by symbols rather than by the accretion of sociology, psychology, music, and all the other impedimenta of realism. *The Trial* has the force of a well-knit play, being conceived dramatically rather than narrationally. It possesses little of the luxurious baggage of the modern novel, such as discourses on time and the past or intellectual and sensuous documentation.

Its greatest stylistic advance over *Amerika* is in the merger of expressionism and psychology. *Amerika* contains too many barren passages depending on a bald, unexciting realism to permit it to rank with *The Trial;* expressionism, except at crucial moments, seems grafted onto the event. In *The Trial* it is internal to the event, assimilated in its very core. This is partly due to K.'s more profound abnormality as compared to Karl's, for expressionism suits the abnormal, since both it and the abnormal specialize in distortion. Here we encroach on the relation between Kafka's dream world and his expressionism:

dreams, it may be said, are expressionistic distortions of the real world to express hidden meanings in patterns which are half-familiar, half-strange. Expressionism and realism entail differing relations between author and audience, which are partly apparent in a comparison of Kafka's first two novels. In realism the relation is familiar even when the style is extremely objective, as in Flaubert. The author is helpful even while pretending to be absent: he narrates to bridge hiatuses in the plot and describes to bridge ellipses in the environment.

The humor, which in *Amerika* was on the whole compassionate, in *The Trial* is sardonic. Here it is diabolic over trifling details during the most dramatic moments. But despite its sardonic tone it is remarkably Jewish: it contains that strange quality of laughter through tears. It is this which endears Joseph K. to the reader. Besides being an ethical epicure he is a quixotic fool. His world is as queer and wonderful as a fairy-tale world and just as full of witches and gnomes; only the good fairies are missing. We marvel at the poetic embroidery and our heads rarely nod; on the contrary our eyes grow ever wider with amazement and disbelief.

One imagines that if Joseph K. had desired a personal motto he would have chosen Goethe's dying words, 'More light'; for his is the tale of the search for light in a world of darkness and torment. How exciting it is: a man seems to be in mortal danger, yet no one knows why. We are disturbed, we grow restless; in the meantime the remarkable narrative, with its fantastic distortions, speeds on. It is all a good deal obscene under the mantle of restraint and decency—how dare the second warder butt Joseph K. with his fat belly?—and we grow a little breathless and queasy. But then we laugh: so Joseph K. thinks a bicycle license can substitute for a birth certificate! How droll! Fight them, we think; tell them off; give them no leeway. These are gangsters: see how they keep the victim in cruel suspense, toying with him, not telling him whether or not they intend to rub him out. And the business of the inspector playing with the candle, the matchbox, the book and the pincushion, arranging and rearranging them, making the candle suggest a phallic symbol: that seems like a sequence out of a film of the 'twenties: the cold toying with inanimate objects paralleling and symbolizing the heartless toying with a very animate victim. How queer K. is with women. He fears them: Is that why they fear him? In his excited state he imagines devils all around him; he fears even the house-porter's son, as if by some fantastic scheme the boy might be a powerful court functionary spying on him; after he learns the boy's true identity he cannot resist turning around for another look.

In many respects Joseph K. resembles Hans Castorp of *The Magic Mountain.* Castorp encourages physical disease, Joseph K. mental disease, through suggestion. Castorp is fascinated by the sanatorium, K. by the court. Castorp likes being ill, K. likes being on trial. Both gain a sense of importance because of their problems. Castorp revels in physical attention as a relief from bourgeois correctness and *sangfroid;* K. revels in moral attention as a relief from being a nonentity, his father's forgotten son. Basically he prefers a trial with the danger of death to a sane and morally mediocre existence. He prefers the distinction of being accused—only the mediocre are never put on trial.

If *The Trial* is deficient in tenderness it is not so in horror. Kafka, an expert in literary horror, has his fling in the chapter called 'The Whipper,' a bit of writing reeking of burning flesh. The experience is calculated to break K.'s spirit by showing him the court's callousness and meticulous adherence to technicality. What has been decreed is just; what exists is good; what is, is right. The chapter underlines K.'s sense of guilt, which is attracted to things not related to him and which needs no causal connections to make it respond. It also emphasizes his sadism, which is his guilt in reverse, acting externally. K.'s willingness to accept guilt for the remotest events is typical of him—and of neurotics. His sense of guilt is nothing passive. It projects itself, it has power and ego. It even projects itself upon situations that K. has not personally experienced. In the final analysis it holds him responsible for all human sufferings and for the creation of the world itself.

Kafka's dream-world emerges excellently in the two chapters devoted to the interrogation chamber. K.'s hysteria results from an inability to cope with his environment. Kafka motivates K.'s condition by realistic means, describing the stale, hot air of the place. He is also speaking symbolically, indicting the chamber for its lack of freedom and enlightenment. The inversion which is the basis of many of Kafka's expressionistic effects is evident in the fact that the court is poverty-stricken, situated in the slums, rather than majestic and regal, a symbol of the state. K., an important functionary in a bank, symbol of wealth and power, is placed on trial by the poor and diseased. All the accused in *The Trial* seem to belong to the economically superior class, while the accusers are of the lower depths. Kafka seems to be implying that it is mainly the upper classes that are neurotic; he seems to be implying an equation between economic and cultural levels and saying that neurosis is a kind of hemophilia of the better fed and educated. In the Europe of his day there was indeed a high correlation between poverty and ignorance, culture and wealth.

What is the nature of the cabala and the cabalists in *The Trial*? In a fragment entitled 'Public Prosecutor' we learn that K. is not as lonely as the rest of the novel would indicate, that he has a close and powerful friend in the figure of Hasterer, a public prosecutor. K. is a member of Hasterer's dining club, which is composed mainly of judges, public prosecutors, and lawyers. But these legal jurists have no connection with the extra-legal court that is hounding K. The distinction between law and mores, which one has suspected all along, is emphasized by Kafka in the fragment, a distinction heightened just before K.'s execution when he refuses the aid of the policeman, symbol of the state. The state protects the pariah, gives him legal assurance; but the underground (prejudice, discrimination) destroys him. The venality of the cabalistic court is suggested by a sentence: 'Between two men who were talking together just inside the door—the one was making with both hands a gesture as if paying out money while the other was looking him sharply in the eye—a hand reached out and seized K.' The motifs of airlessness, fogginess, and filth recur in the novel with a contrapuntal effect; with them is presented the motif of darkness (obscurantism), as seen in the anachronistic and widespread use of candles. The nocturnal creatures of the court are like gnomes, dwarfs, bats, moles, yet it is they who try the inhabitants of the upper world. The conflict between reason and the unconscious, between law and disorder, between science and the irrational, is basically Kafka's great theme. K. is the man of vision in the land of the blind; to the catacomb creatures his sight is disease; they torment and slay him. He himself ironically is ashamed of his eyes and half-wishes to put them out.

What is the court but a drumhead court? The proceedings are not public, the charge-sheets inaccessible. Fantastic and purely fictional as this seems, it was unfortunately prophetic, for in the fascist nations the irrational became a political creed, instituting such courts as tried Joseph K., with similar if more efficient results. But what was accomplished by force by the fascists is accomplished by suggestion by the court. There is no hint of force in *The Trial*, no mention of seizure, imprisonment, punishment. Tragically enough the accused do not concern themselves with punishment; they are so trapped by means that they have no energy to consider ends.

The Trial is Kafka's portrayal of the conflict between the son and the father. The battle with the father in *Amerika* has become the battle with the group father in *The Trial.* Joseph K., unlike Karl Rossmann, cannot be stoked emotionally, but he can be stoked intellectually; he has devised no defense against intellectual hocus-pocus. His neurosis has moved from the affectional to the intellectual level of expression. He is incapable of ambivalence toward males except in an intellectual sense. All hints of homosexuality, through caresses and fondling, are conspicuous by their absence. The father now browbeats the son in terms of social codes. His attack is equated with the attack of authoritarian elements in society upon the intellectually and morally superior outcasts. What in *Amerika* was a personal conflict has now been broadened into a conflict between types of human beings. Kafka does not hesitate to appropriate for himself the progressive, enlightening role, while giving to his father the role of reactionary darkness. The symbols have been broadened, the allegory generalized; and as a consequence the autobiography is more elusive.

The Trial is Joseph K.'s education for death. The task of the father is to slay the son. The task of the son is to slay himself. The destruction of the victim proceeds artistically, in such a manner as to bring most shame upon him. He is manipulated to the point where he himself approves of it.

The symbolism of the warders' black suits and K.'s black coat is obvious. The guilt of the accused is presumed. The cabalists never doubt the omnipotence of their system. At first K., certain of his innocence, expresses himself forcefully; but soon he is infected with a slavish masochism. When he is told the inspector wants him the command itself is welcome to him. 'At last,' he shouts, an expression at once of his love of friction and of his fascination for forces inimical to him.

When K. asks by what authority they question him he is put out by what he calls sheer nonsense, yet is impressed by that very nonsense all the same. Just at those times when he shines by his logic some ridiculous action throws him off balance. This motif is a satire on the futility and tenuousness of the verbal magic of the pariah. Whenever K. is on the verge of challenging the cabala he is seduced by a sudden change of pace. The warders cry out that he cannot see the inspector without getting dressed. He replies: 'Let me alone, damn you! If you grab me out of bed, you can't expect to find me all dressed up in my best suit.' '"This doesn't help you any," said the warders, who as soon as K. raised his voice always grew quite calm, indeed almost rueful, and thus contrived either to confuse him or to some extent bring him to his senses.' They play with the neurotic, knowing he is helpless because of his ambivalence.

Since males torment him, K. seeks solace with females. He is full of gratitude toward Frau Grubach because she makes light of his arrest. 'Will she take my hand? The Inspector wouldn't do it,' he thinks. But out of embarrassment she forgets to take it—a crucial rebuff. He represses his anger but it bursts out when with 'sudden fury' he rails at her for making unkind remarks about Fräulein Bürstner, as if he knew the latter intimately and had to defend her honor. Frau Grubach is regular, sensible, rooted. Her avoidance of his hand convinces him more than ever that he is a pariah.

He has no special desire to see Fräulein Bürstner and hardly remembers how she looks, yet he wishes to talk to her and is exasperated by her tardiness. When he sees her in the hallway he whispers her name through the chink of his door. 'It sounded like a prayer, not like a summons.' It is K.'s prayer to be accepted by the female, the mother, in order to find protection from the male. He behaves so queerly that Fräulein Bürstner regrets having let him into her room. She submits to his caresses, but as though she were submitting to a beast. His further fruitless wooing of her in Chapter IV is heightened by the formation of two pairs—Montag and Bürstner, and Montag and Lanz. The second pair is even more damaging than the first, for it emphasizes K.'s mateless state. Lanz is a 'better' man than he is—tall, tanned, his movements easy, a captain with a uniform, one of the belongers.

K.'s first major show of strength in his battle with the fathers occurs in the chapter entitled 'First Interrogation,' in which he challenges the examining magistrate and the right and left groups of the lower court. He expends most of his strength and self-assurance in this encounter. His speech is full of damaging points, yet it is also replete with whistlings in the dark. It reminds one of Karl Rossmann's two long speeches. It contains the same mixture of prolixity, forcefulness, and boasting.

K.'s uncle is the father as vulgarian Babbitt. He resembles Hans Castorp's uncle in *The Magic Mountain*. He comes from the flatland of the country to the sanatorium-city, blusters awhile, then leaves abruptly. But whereas Castorp's uncle is a burgher who wishes Hans to return to the fold from the Davos-wilderness of bohemianism, K.'s uncle wants K. to remain to fight his case. Castorp, like Mann, is always the man of good conscience playing the bohemian, while K., like Kafka, is the true pariah. K.'s uncle readily accepts the cabala of the court. He is not concerned with theoretical justice but with political maneuvers designed to avoid a scandal. His function is to increase K.'s hysteria. He is a member of the tribe of irrationals. 'The first thing to grasp, Uncle,' says K., 'is that this is not a case before an ordinary court.' 'That's bad,' says the uncle. 'How?' asks K. 'I mean that it's bad,' the uncle repeats. The uncle insinuates that K.'s brain is foggy. He says,

'Looking at you, one would almost believe the old saying: "A litigant always loses."' K. replies that there is no use in his getting excited, adding that it would be better for him to remain in the city to push his case more energetically. To this the uncle eagerly assents, since the more strenuously K. fights, the sooner he is lost.

In Chapter VII Kafka's satire on the technique of hair-splitting reaches its zenith. With Huld, as with Titorelli and the priest, every statement has its negation, every motion its counter-motion. Thus Huld stands still while seeming to go forward. K.'s torture is caused by the disparity between the apparent motion (hope) and the real stasis (despair). Huld is an international type, the typical bureaucrat, the sometimes obsequious and sometimes arrogant apologist for the irrational and the *status quo,* who makes capital out of the weakest sections of his theology, out of contradictions, cultural lags and reactionary dogma. Ironically enough, for all his insights and passion for reform, K. is the product of the court culture as represented in the bank. He is the victim of his own philosophy of discipline. A more bohemian victim would let matters go as they pleased. But K. refuses to allow the irrational to be itself. His is a tragedy of the middle man, who cannot belong yet is not extremist enough to scorn the belongers.

The Trial is a fantasy of indirection, in which Kafka's obsession with his wounds deprives the novel of that balance which makes for epic conflict. Nowhere in the novel (or in Kafka's wider world) is there the figure of the saintly skeptic or noble humanist. To have introduced even one such type in *The Trial,* perhaps as a friend or mentor of K., would have lent the book an epic balance lacking in it. As it stands, the conflict is between oceans of darkness and a flickering candlelight.

The tale of the doorkeeper is *The Trial* in miniature. It illustrates Kafka's method of illumination, which consists of a slowly growing stock of information followed by brilliant flashes of allegorical insight. K. is prepared for death by the symbolism of the slain Christ in the altar-piece. The suggestion is that Christ, like K., was a pariah, and that he was murdered by such people as the knight, symbol of physical force. The priest is calm; he knows his power over the suggestible K. K. flies toward his persecutor, doomed to a flatulent articulation beneath which lies an appalling silence. He is incapable of asking elementary questions, such as: What are you doing in the cathedral? How did you know my name? How did you know I·was coming here? What have you, a priest, to do with the court? What would you do if I walked out now, refusing to listen to you? His slavishness before social conventions is Egyptian. It is characteristic of the Europe between 1870 and the outbreak of the First World War. It is not accidental that the man who approaches the doorkeeper is a man from the country, an outsider, and that the doorkeeper seems strange to him, as if he were a member of a foreign tribe, with his 'furred robe, huge pointed nose and long, thin, Tartar beard.' The latter solves the problem of immigration by verbal mesmerism. The barbarian defeats the intellectual at his own game. K.'s instinct that the doorkeeper deluded the man is sound and his anger justified, for to act according to the letter of the law in the presence of suffering is immoral. The priest soon smothers him with sophistry. The tale of the doorkeeper is among other things an allegory of inquisition; it demonstrates what is possible in the way of cruelty when form is idolized to the detriment of spirit. When K. says, 'A melancholy conclusion. It turns lying into a universal principle,' he expresses succinctly one of the most disheartening of modern facts: the exploitation of the excuse of necessity for the subordination of truth, and the sanctification of means at the expense of ends.

Thus ends the battle between K. and the fathers. The

execution is only a matter of convenience. Thus ends also the substance of a most prophetic book. The current interest in Kafka is not unconnected with Kafka's prophetic talent. Fascism was only a tactical battle in the war between darkness and light. The conflict between K. and the fathers was such a battle in the symbolic and personal sphere.

We have seen that *Amerika,* on the symbolic level, is the tale of the sexual education of a Kafka protagonist and that it is composed of three progressive sexual parts: the narcissistic, the platonic, and the heterosexual. We have seen also that maturity and happiness are there viewed in terms of a heterosexual adjustment. This pattern, sketched in the first novel, is amplified in Kafka's trilogy. The narcissistic stage is represented by *Amerika,* the platonic by *The Trial* and the heterosexual by *The Castle.*

In *Amerika* the dominant tone is homosexual: Karl continues to be exposed to crushes. In *The Trial* Joseph K. nowhere seems to be domesticated or even to have a love affair. In *The Castle* the domestic factor is overwhelming. There are numerous family situations, and K. achieves a domestic relationship with Frieda.

The Castle is more mellow than *The Trial.* Its epic style and classic mood, its sense of space, its calm prose have a powerful effect. It is Kafka's pastorale, his summing up.

It is not an exaggeration to say that Kafka's works—and his novels in particular—are anthropological studies. He deals with a culture, offering a perspective on it. His isolation gave him startling cultural insights. His antagonists are philistines. Like the peoples of all cultures who have no perspective on themselves, they identify local custom with universal laws of behavior. But what seems universal to the insiders is clearly only provincial to the protagonist-outsider. Kafka's protagonists are dangerous aliens. The insiders are the only true believers. It is they who have access to divine truth; the outsider is conversant only with evil, error, and the devil.

Kafka does not merely present the problem of the outsider. He makes value judgments on it. He condemns him to death because he behaves so rigidly in his efforts to belong. And he satirizes the insiders because, in their wretched blindness, they persecute the outsider.

The problem of the alien is a function of all periods of intense migration, of interpenetration of cultures. It is particularly acute for the Jew. Kafka's outsider is a modern Everyman. We are all Jews today, wanderers and heathens in a world exploding under the impact of those myths of necessity and the absolute which characterize western civilization's preoccupation with the competitive and acquisitive spirit.

Kafka's world may also be interpreted fruitfully in terms of the conflict between an outmoded, sterile classicism and a usurping, youthful romanticism. The insistence on considering social laws as preordained rather than relative, which is so basic to Kafka's antagonists, is typical of classicism. The insistence of the protagonists on defending their individual rights on the basis of logic is part of the large romantic pattern.

In *Amerika* the cabala is personal, a father imago. In *The Trial* it is partially social, with an emphasis on males. In *The Castle* it is society in general. The father is not simply prejudice, superstition and irrationality but the framework of society itself. He is no longer the avenging father but the father as supremely indifferent.

The process of K.'s conversion to the lowest of the low among the villagers and of his acceptance of this conversion is one of the leading themes of *The Castle*. K. is masochistically attracted to defeat. There is no question of the castle's being unattainable. It is only unattainable to K. because he is compulsive and weary.

[118]

One of the chief agents in his conversion is Klamm, the important father surrogate. K., unduly impressed by parental authority, readily accepts the fiction of Klamm's power. He desires from Klamm a parental blessing for his marriage to Frieda. In addition, he hopes through Klamm to move toward his desired conflict with the castle. Eventually he intends to battle the count, the primal father, yet this prospect is so distant that it is barely mentioned in the novel. But in a remarkable passage occurring in the opening of Chapter VIII, in which K. waits vainly for Klamm at the latter's sledge, the symbolism is unusually transparent.

When K. looked at the Castle, often it seemed to him as if he were observing someone who sat quietly there gazing in front of him, not lost in thought and so oblivious of everything, but free and untroubled, as if he were alone with nobody to observe him, and yet must notice that he was observed, and all the same remained with his calm not even slightly disturbed; and really—one did not know whether it was cause or effect—the gaze of the observer could not remain concentrated there, but slid away.

This imperturbability, this lack of self-consciousness, is exactly what Kafka admired in his father.

The Barnabas family, which collectively has the same role in *The Castle* that Joseph K. has in *The Trial*, is attacked and destroyed by the cabala. It is not aggressive like K. but passive like Joseph K. Found guilty of challenging the cabala, it has been excommunicated. Like Joseph K., it is part of the culture that condemns it. It is innocent of a specific charge, yet is convinced of its guilt because of a general burden of guilt. Like Joseph K., it destroys itself.

In its history of woe K. sees proof of the castle's power. Thus the Barnabas family is an important agent in his conversion. Olga is completely cabalistic, convinced of the justice of the family's punishment. She is intent on appeasing the gods, uncertain only in regard to the crucial sacrifice. As for K., although he possesses the perspective of the outsider, he nevertheless accepts the notion that the castle's authority is real and good, submitting himself unquestionably to all the moral blindness such an assumption entails. He thereby reveals his neurotic shortcomings.

Amalia was condemned not because 'it's all engineered from the Castle,' as Olga claims, but because neither she nor the family was able to behave as if innocent. The punishment, although suggested by the villagers, was self-inflicted. K. asks: 'And where do you see in all this the influence of the Castle?' Olga's reply is: 'We all knew that no definite punishment would be visited on us. We were only shunned. By the village and by the Castle. But while we couldn't help noticing the ostracism of the village, the Castle gave us no sign. Of course we had had no sign of favor from the Castle in the past, so how could we notice the reverse?'

She asserts that the villagers were only waiting for the family to resume its normal life so that they might accept it into the community again. She says, '. . . a happy ending to the whole story would have pleased everybody best.' The villagers, alarmed by the family's acquiescence, are convinced of its guilt. 'They saw that we hadn't the strength to shake ourselves clear of the scandal and they were irritated . . . if we had triumphed they would have honoured us correspondingly, but since we failed they turned what had only been a temporary measure into a final resolve, and cut us off from the community for ever. . ."

The family's efforts to prove its guilt in order to have a right to petition the castle for a pardon, fantastic as it seems, is but a logical step in its progressive neurosis.

It is unfortunate that the English and American editions of *The Castle,* like those of *Amerika* and *The Trial,* should be mutilated forms of the originals.* In the case of *The Castle* fully two and a half chapters are missing, half of Chapter xviii and both Chapters xix and xx. These contain some of the best writing in the novel. They bring to a supreme pitch Kafka's satire on bureaucracy and cabalism. His sardonic humor at the expense of the bureaucratic mind, which was hinted at in his earlier work, has its final orchestral fortissimo here. The castle is represented as an enormous bureaucracy of males, a hideous paper-work structure enmeshed and bewitched by a dreamlike red tape of legendary proportions. The emphasis on records, the ultra-meticulousness, the enormous hierarchy, the difficulty of communication—these are all burlesques of the really terrifying bureaucracy of the Austro-Hungarian Empire.

The following chapter presents an aspect of Kafka that seemingly contradicts all I have hitherto said, an aspect involving nothing less than the discovery of a secret 'key' to the novels, a key as comprehensive, deliberate and real as the Odysseus key to Joyce's *Ulysses*. The contradiction, I am convinced, is illusory, existing only between separate universes of discourse.

* The reason for this mutilation seems to be that the publishers based the translations upon early German editions of the novels; but why this situation has not been remedied since 1935, when the full versions appeared in the collected German edition, remains unclear.

The Secret Meaning of *The Castle**

EVER since its appearance *The Castle* has been the subject of numerous exegeses, most of them extremely general and none very convincing. An assumption basic to all of them is that Kafka's effects were intuitive and his symbolism unconscious. Another is that it is impossible to resolve the novel's discrepancies and that the fundamental theme of the work is so allusive and vague as to permit many keys and endless argument. I hope to prove that *The Castle* contains a cohesive and deliberate pattern of symbols and a cryptic meaning whose existence is indubitable and that it is no longer permissible to argue vaguely concerning its meaning.

My findings are fourfold:

1. *The Castle* contains a web of symbols that are mainly sexual in nature—those symbols common to dreams, folklore, and the unconscious as discussed by the psychoanalytic movement, especially by Freud, Jung, and Stekel.

2. It is a literary panorama of the states of consciousness as discovered by the psychoanalytic movement.

---

* In the following two chapters the novels will be discussed in chronologically reversed order. Kafka's secret methods developed progressively and are easier to follow in the last novel, where they are full-blown, than in the first two, where they are more or less tentative.

This analysis is by no means exhaustive. Only the general lines of symbolic pattern are indicated. It is doubtful that a truly exhaustive analysis can be made of a work so entirely allusive and creative.

3. It presents in detail the dynamics of the Oedipus complex.

4. It contains a web of nomenclatural symbolism.

The influence of psychoanalysis on Kafka is hardly surprising. By 1912, when Kafka 'broke through' artistically, the psychoanalytic movement was in full swing, exploring the mythological, anthropological, and artistic ramifications of its discoveries. Freud and Kafka were produced by identical cultural factors: both were Jews, both were born in Central Europe (Freud in Moravia, now, like Bohemia, part of Czechoslovakia), both struggled against the shibboleths of the Gentile Austro-Hungarian Empire; both were irregular, both were skeptical, both were intent on discovering the reality and through it the possibility of human amelioration.

In peopling the depth psychology Kafka mirrored his own culture. He made bureaucrats out of the gentlemen of the unconscious and hypersensitive moralists, resembling philistines, of his preconscious characters. He visualized the unconscious as the great authority, with feudal powers. His choice of the castle as the chief symbol of the novel was by no means accidental. The fact that he did not select a religious symbol (such as cathedral or chapel) to represent woman, mother, and the unconscious is indicative of his non-religious position.

Kafka's symbols and hidden meanings manipulate the reader's unconscious. They are part of a hypnotic program. One comprehends him, realizes him, without necessarily understanding him. His cool style effectively disguises his potions. Reading him, one moves close to the unconscious. That is why we are disturbed, why we wish to resist. His symbols and meanings are interconnected. They possess a fluid significance, on many levels, some contradictory. The problem of the individual *vs.* authority is also the problem of the son *vs.* the father and the conscious *vs.* the unconscious.

[123]

On the social level the villagers' belief in the existence and power of the castle is superstitious; on the psychological it is based on reality, the dominance of the unknown unconscious. In one context K. is a hero battling irrational authority and demanding 'inalienable' rights and a brand of justice based on reason and logic. In another he is sick and blind, seeking to find and enjoy the very things that in the previous context he wishes to destroy.

The Castle is a modern myth in which man's tragedy is his fruitless quest for his unconscious and for the resolution of his neurotic torment there. K. is a mixture of Oedipus and Hamlet. He is doomed merely to seek to do the very things that Oedipus with a brash hand did. He is denied the pleasure of possessing Jocasta and the cosmic penance of tearing out his eyes. He is doomed to be an Oedipus just short of realization, with the eternal failure of a Sisyphus.

1. SYMBOLISM

There are two types of symbolism in The Castle: *mythical symbolism * and symbolic action.*

Mythical symbolism. A castle, like a village, town, citadel, and fortress, is a symbol of woman and mother. A count is a father symbol, like emperor, king, and president.† The count's permission is necessary for K. to enter the castle; i.e. the father's permission is necessary for the son to possess his mother incestuously. Land too is a symbol of woman and mother, as indicated by the expression 'mother earth.' A land

---

* I have applied this term to those dream symbols which psychoanalysis has described as archetypal and phylogenetic. While it is true that mythical symbols may be found in any fictional work, in Kafka's work they are overwhelmingly predominant. It is not true that all objects fall into the categories of male and female symbols and that therefore Kafka's symbols are accidentals.

† The symbol of Venus ($\female$) and the symbol of Mars ($\male$) will henceforth be used to denote female and male symbols respectively.

surveyor is therefore one who measures the mother—the incestuous implication is obvious. K.'s surveying apparatus, an obvious symbol of his masculinity, never arrives; i.e. he is not adequate sexually, although he has unusual sexual drives. K. telephones the castle (the old-fashioned telephone is a male symbol) and later discovers that there is no real connection with the castle. The lack of sexual connection is an important theme of the novel.

When K. embarks on his first village walk he pauses near the church (♀), a chapel (♀) with barnlike (♀) additions. He flings a snowball at a window (♀); a door (♀) opens, a plank (♂) is shoved out to rescue him from the snow. He enters the house of the tanner Lasemann (probably from the German *lass,* weak, since the tanner is described as weary and weak). Filled with steam, it is the scene of washing and splashing (water symbolizes birth or rebirth), with children loudly crying and with a woman nursing an infant at her breast. Coitus is performed symbolically by two men bathing in a wooden tub (♀) 'as wide as two beds.' The men stamp and roll (rhythmic and violent acts symbolize coitus). The children, trying to draw close, are frustrated by 'mighty splashes of water'—i.e. social taboo. One of the men, with his mouth hanging open (♀), showers drops of warm water on K.'s face. 'From a large opening (♀), the only one in the back wall, a pale snowy light came in, apparently from the courtyard, and gave a gleam as of silk (♀) to the dress of a woman . . . almost reclining in a high arm-chair.' Emphasis on materials is a constant motif, since materials (from *mater,* mother) is a female symbol.

K. dozes and awakes refreshed. He 'poked with his stick (♂) here and there' and 'noted that he was physically the biggest man in the room.' His courage rises when he approaches female symbols. ' "I say," cried K. suddenly—they were already near the church (♀), the inn (♀) was not far off, and K. felt he could risk something—"I'm surprised that you have the nerve to drive me round on your own responsibility; are you allowed to do that?" ' Again Gerstäcker's mouth falls open, displaying 'a few isolated teeth' (♂). K.'s assistants have black pointed beards (♂) and tight-fitting clothes. (Their clothes resemble uniforms and uniforms symbolize nudity.) K.'s coitus with Frieda is preceded by many sexual symbols: the uniforms of the Herrenhof peasants, the peephole (♀) through which K. sees Klamm, Klamm himself, Frieda's 'low-cut cream-colored blouse,' the leather bag (♀) hanging at her girdle, from which she draws the small piece of wood to stop up the peephole (wood is a female symbol used here as a male symbol because of its shape), the peasant dance around Olga, Frieda's whip (♂), et cetera.

At the superintendent's K. witnesses a mass of symbols: the superintendent's gouty leg (♂), the candles (♂), cabinet (♀), shed (♀), chest (♀), the rolls (♂) of paper (♂) documents (paper is derived from papyrus, a long-stemmed plant with a spray on top). The Bridge Inn landlady has retained three (♂) * keepsakes from Klamm, who sent for her three (♂) times. In the schoolroom there are gymnastic apparatus (♂), wood (♀), shed (♀), sausage (♂), stove (♀), candle (♂), and cat (♀).

The celebration of the Fire Brigade festival is a phallic fest, the fire engine symbolizing the phallus. The male symbolism is powerful. The celebration occurred about three (♂) years ago, on the third (♂) of July, and Amalia's father was third (♂) in command of the brigade. Sortini leaped over the engine shaft (♂) to approach Amalia. Trumpets (♂) are prominent. Amalia's letter from Sortini is the third (♂) and last delivered during the novel's progress, K. having received two others from Klamm. Amalia is the third (♂) woman

* According to psychoanalysis, the sacred number three is a mythical symbol of the whole male genitalia.

whom we see in a sexual relation to the castle officials, the Bridge Inn landlady and Frieda being the other two. Female symbols are also present, in particular the necklace of garnets (♀) which the Bridge Inn landlady gave Olga and which Olga gave to Amalia. Coming from a former mistress of Klamm, the necklace was an important gift, a symbol of fertility. Olga impulsively conferred it on her sister because she unconsciously understood Amalia's personal tragedy and hoped by the gift to make her normal.

The Herrenhof landlady is obsessed with the idea of clothes. Kafka emphasizes the material (♀) of her dresses. K. comes to a secret agreement with Pepi. He will knock three (♂) times for admittance.

Symbolic action. An interesting paragraph concerns K.'s memory of having climbed a wall in his boyhood. He recalls a church (♀) partly surrounded by a high wall (♂) in the market place of his native town.

Very few boys had managed to climb that wall, and for some time K., too, had failed. It was not curiosity which had urged them on. The graveyard had been no mystery to them. They had often entered it through a small wicket-gate, it was only the smooth high wall that they had wanted to conquer. But one morning—the empty, quiet market-place had been flooded with sunshine, when had K. ever seen it like that either before or since?—he had succeeded in climbing it with astonishing ease; at a place where he had already slipped down many a time he had clambered with a small flag between his teeth right to the top at the first attempt.

Climbing symbolizes coitus. The failure of the boys may have resulted from the unwillingness of their partners or from various psychic or physical causes. The episode alludes to K.'s first sexual success, which was unexpectedly easy after much difficulty. Its memory succors him while he is dragged on the arm of Barnabas through the snowy night. Barnabas takes him to his house, not to the castle—i.e. to domesticity rather than incest. But K. regards the castle as his true home, since that is where his 'parents' reside. He ponders: 'So it was only Barnabas who was at home, not he himself.'

The incident of Klamm's sledge (♀) symbolizes an act of onanism.

He opened the wide door (♀) and could without more ado have drawn a flask (♀) out of the side pocket (♀) which was fastened to the inside of the door; but now that it was open he felt an impulse which he could not withstand to go inside the sledge; all he wanted was to sit there for a minute. He slipped inside. The warmth . . . was extraordinary . . . although the door, which K. did not dare to close, was wide open . . . one could turn and stretch on every side, and always one sank into softness and warmth.

K. is stupefied by this womblike warmth. Finally he reaches into the pocket of the closed door (the forbidden one) and pulls out a flask. The brandy is like a perfume, sweet and caressing. 'Can this be brandy?' he asks himself doubtfully. 'Yes, strangely enough it was brandy, and burned and warmed him. How wonderfully it was transformed in drinking out of something which seemed hardly more than a sweet perfume into a drink fit for a coachman!' But now he is regretful. ' "Can it be?" K. asked himself as if self-reproachfully, and took another sip.'

Suddenly the electric lights (of his conscience) blaze on and he is caught in the act by Momus, a father surrogate. 'This is unheard of,' says Momus, pushing his hat (♂) back on his forehead. K. retrieves his cap (♂) from the sledge and notices 'with discomfort' that the brandy is dripping from the footboard. K. refuses to accompany Momus and Momus 'ran the tip of his tongue round his slightly-parted lips,' a sexual gesture. Momus orders the horses stabled, i.e. the passions locked up. He and the coachman disappear. Finally

[128]

the electric lights go off. Then it seems to K. that 'these people' have broken off all relations with him. He had 'won a freedom such as hardly anybody else had ever succeeded in winning.' Yet he feels that there is nothing more senseless and hopeless than this freedom. This is perhaps a reference to the 'freedom of the artist' on which Kafka insisted in his relations with F.B., and which he finally found to be utterly sterile if divorced from the main stream of existence.

He wrenches himself free of this 'freedom' and returns to the Herrenhof. There he meets Gardana, Momus, and Pepi. A brandy he orders from Pepi he finds undrinkable. He desires more of the Klamm-brandy, which is sweet, but Pepi, as if frowning on onanism, curtly says she has no other kind.

2. THE DEPTH PSYCHOLOGY

The outside world, from which K. originates, symbolizes the conscious mind. It does not figure importantly in The Castle *because* The Castle *is the tale of the quest for the unconscious by someone who has reached the preconscious. The village is the preconscious and the castle the unconscious.* *The village, like the preconscious, is the basis of morality, normality, conscience and fecundity. It contains the two teachers, dream-symbols of conscience and morality. The castle, like the unconscious, is primitive, irrational, and infantile. Identified with it are Klamm, god of sex (libido), Erlanger, god of dreams, and Bürgel, god of sleep.*

Kafka describes the unconscious by describing the castle tower. It has windows with 'a somewhat maniacal glitter' and battlements that are chaotic and childish, 'irregular, broken, fumbling, as if designed by the trembling or careless hand of a child. . .' The castle gentlemen are psychic messengers connecting the unconscious with the preconscious. The Bridge

---

* Freud's concept of id, ego, and super-ego appeared too late to be utilized by Kafka in *The Castle*.

Inn is the frontier between the conscious and the preconscious, the Herrenhof between the preconscious and unconscious. K. is permitted only in the bar of the Herrenhof—beyond that is the beginning of the unconscious. The Herrenhof is reserved exclusively for gentlemen from the castle. Over it, as a mark of distinction, flies a flag with the count's colors. The Herrenhof landlord 'seemed to have hardly anything in common with the village, even although his dark clothes looked like a peasant's finery.' Like the landlord, the peasants of the Herrenhof look different from those in the Bridge Inn. 'They were more neatly and uniformly dressed in coarse yellowish-grey cloth, with loose jackets and tightly-fitting trousers.' The Bridge Inn landlady is the censor between the conscious and preconscious, just as her counterpart in the Herrenhof is the censor between the preconscious and unconscious. (Censors in the form of females and landladies are sly Kafkian comments on women.) Gardana (from the German *Garde*, guard) tries unceasingly to prevent K. from making his descent to the unconscious and says it was only her husband's carelessness which got K. into the village, 'for I was tired to death on that evening.' K.'s efforts to reach the castle cause her great unhappiness. She 'can't work, lies in bed and sighs and complains all the time,' according to her husband. K. thinks of her (after his interview with Momus): 'An intriguing nature, acting blindly, it seemed, like the wind, according to strange and remote behests which one could never guess at.' She is as strange to him as his preconscious and stranger still when she is in the Herrenhof, in contact with the unconscious. The Herrenhof landlady has a 'positively morbid determination to be refined' and she exercises a kind of petty tyranny, 'thanks to her indefatigable yet femininely insinuating zeal.'

K.'s interview with the superintendent illuminates the symbolic pattern. Official intercourse with the authorities is for K. easy—i.e. it is easy to confront the preconscious. K.

thinks of the 'admirable autonomy of the service, which one divined to be peculiarly effective precisely where it was not visibly present'—a reference to the hidden unconscious and its power. The superintendent is gouty, a symbol, together with the many limping men of the village, of the limping quality of the preconscious, which strains to mediate between the conscious and the unconscious. K. thinks of the village authorities: 'They seemed literally to bear every burden, one could lay everything on their shoulders and remain free and untouched oneself'—an accurate picture of the preconscious. The superintendent enlightens K. on the operations within the castle, a bureaucracy of conflicting impulses in which miscalculations may arise but not in important matters. The preconscious, on the other hand, is pictured as bathed in a perpetual twilight: snow obscures the village and there are always lanterns and candles about. K. is forbidden to look for his paper because he is not yet a resident of the preconscious. The assistants, however, belong to the preconscious (they merely imitate the real assistants, who would belong to the unconscious, since their function as testicles is to carry libido); therefore, unable to disturb the superintendent yet capable of disturbing K., they are allowed to rummage through the papers. The superintendent goes on at length about the castle. Messages from the castle to the village sometimes go astray, in which case a desperate search is instituted. K.'s own quest is caused by a message going astray from the unconscious. When the superintendent inquires if the story bores K. the latter replies that it amuses him. But the superintendent asserts that his purpose is not to amuse and he is sincere, a fact which K. does not understand. K. says (quite psychoanalytically): 'It only amuses me because it gives me an insight into the ludicrous bungling which in certain circumstances may decide the life of a human being.'

Of the assistants he rightly says, 'they might as well have

fallen from the sky, for all the thought that was spent in choosing them.' When he poses a direct question concerning the castle he is rebuffed with the village taboo. 'She comes, of course, from the Castle?' he asks regarding Brunswick's wife. The superintendent reacts quickly. 'The superintendent looked at the clock, poured some medicine into a spoon, and gulped at it hastily.' K. receives no reply. His paper is never found—a symbol of his lost sexuality.

The superintendent differentiates between his own nature and an official's, like Sordini's. Sordini is a primitive, belonging to the unconscious; the superintendent, a member of the comparatively civilized preconscious, is a gentleman. The verbal exchange between Sordini and the superintendent is amusing as well as symbolic. The unconscious is always correct, it always operates in the interests of the libido; therefore the superintendent says sincerely, 'It's a working principle of the Head Bureau that the very possibility of error must be ruled out of account,' yet it is clear that the psychic mechanism in K.'s case has misfunctioned, the control officials have permitted an error to slip in. The superintendent relates his debate with Sordini over the responsibility for the error. The case was finally brought to trial in the village (preconscious) and Sordini was temporarily defeated (repressed). The administrative apparatus is extremely delicate. An arbitrary decision may occur in a flash when least expected. 'It's as if the administrative apparatus were unable any longer to bear the tension, the year-long irritation caused by the same affair—probably trivial in itself—and had hit upon the decision by itself, without the assistance of the officials.' The decision, in psychoanalytic terms, takes the form of neurotic symptoms, such as compulsive acts which relieve the tension. The amazing thing about the decisions, the superintendent explains, 'is that one learns too late about them and so in the meantime keeps on still passionately canvassing things that were decided long ago.' This corresponds to the free-floating anxiety typical of neurosis, the need to reach down and pluck out the thorn in one's psyche. K. ends the interview by announcing that he wants no act of favor from the castle but only his rights. These are the words of a man dependent only on the barren conscious mind. They indicate how much K. has yet to learn.

The village taboo against incest is demonstrated forcibly. When K. encounters the male schoolteacher and children, the teacher inquires if he is looking at the castle, 'with an inflection that denoted disapproval of K.'s occupation.' K. admits that he is. '"You don't like the Castle?" returned the teacher quickly.' K. is taken aback. 'Strangers never do,' the teacher enlarges, as if hoping that K. too does not like it. When K. mentions the count, the teacher retorts in French, 'Please remember that there are innocent children present,' alluding to the incest taboo. K. is disconcerted. He is weary, having made a long journey to the village. This journey alludes to his coming death, since journey symbolizes death. When he walks in the direction of the castle he is defeated by his inhibition against incest; he breaks into a sweat and stops. He begins to realize that the castle (unconscious) is not easily accessible.

When he elicits from Brunswick's wife the fact that she is from the castle (and therefore a mother surrogate) he is instantly escorted outside by the two men at Lasemann's, who fear his incestuous intentions. Left alone in the street, K. thinks, 'A fine setting for a fit of despair, if I were only standing here by accident instead of design,' despairing because he has been rejected by heterosexuality. There follows the meeting with Gerstäcker, the coachman and Charon type. When K. asks to be taken to the castle, Gerstäcker unhesitatingly replies, 'I won't take you there.' The latter also refuses to ride with K., for riding symbolizes coitus. He insists that K. ride, the he perform normal coitus even if only symbolically. The ironic and profound equation of coitus and death in this common symbol of riding is found in mythology. K. hears a bell ringing up in the castle.

The Castle above them, which K. had hoped to reach that very day, was already beginning to grow dark, and retreated again into the distance. But as if to give him a parting sign till their next encounter a bell began to ring merrily up there, a bell which for at least a second made his heart palpitate, for its tone was menacing, too, as if it threatened him with the fulfillment of his vague desire.

The possibility of the fulfillment of his desire is a threat to him, since it involves incest and death.

Pepi (addition) is a creature of the unconscious who has moved into the preconscious to replace Frieda. She represents Kafka's acknowledgment of the psychoanalytic postulate that ideas may move with a limited freedom back and forth between the unconscious and preconscious. She is vindictive, insolent, incompetent, and infantile—characteristics satirizing her sudden displacement from the violent unconscious up into the comparatively reasonable preconscious. She despises Frieda for her preconscious qualities of reticence and restraint. As a member of the unconscious, she has knowledge of K.'s sexual deficiencies; that is why she says laughingly, 'That's so,' when K. asks, 'You mean that I should be proud to have won such a reticent girl?' K. realizes that Pepi possesses something of importance to him. He stares at her greedily. 'It's against orders for the light to be on,' Pepi says and switches it off into the darkness proper to the unconscious.

K. refuses to be examined by Momus. The examination seems suspiciously like a sexual one, with Gardana there to bear witness against him. He fails to understand that he must accept Klamm as an end, not as a means, in order to reach the castle and resolve his Oedipus fixation. The interview with Momus underscores K.'s middle position between Momus and the landlady, between the unconscious and the preconscious. It is a tense one for him. The landlady advises him sincerely, but he rejects her advice as irrational, failing to perceive that it is coherent in its own universe of discourse. When he leaves he tells the landlord, 'I didn't let myself be examined,' cheers himself by a joke and steps into the darkness.

Amalia's punishment resulted from her rejection of her unconscious. The fluid relations between the preconscious and the unconscious discussed by Freud is mentioned by Olga when she says, 'Of course we're all supposed to belong to the Castle, and there's supposed to be no gulf between us, and nothing to be bridged over. . .' But in important things this is not true, she adds. She speaks of her father's attempts to persuade the castle of his guilt and thereby exonerate Amalia and she points out that the family's connection with the castle —Sortini—has been destroyed, i.e. the repression of the impulse set it free in the unconscious beyond the control of the preconscious. The father's efforts were hopeless, as well as injurious to the family. They were efforts to establish his guilt and as such were both tragic and humorous. He sensed his guilt as the object of Amalia's desire but he could not prove it. He sought atonement in sackcloth and ashes, slowly destroying himself.

Olga notes that only the whole authority, not a single official, can pardon, then adds, 'apparently even the authority can only condemn and not pardon'—i.e. the unconscious is incapable of negation, which Freud and other psychoanalysts have asserted. The irrationality of the unconscious is humorously portrayed by the odd goings and comings of the castle officials. Minor impulses, moving between the two mental spheres and having their roots in the unconscious, are the castle servants, who are well-behaved in the castle but wild in the Herrenhof, 'seeing that the Castle regulations aren't fully binding on them in the village. . .' Olga speaks of her efforts

[135]

to reach the castle through the servants, and of Amalia's aloofness. Amalia, actively repressing her desires, cannot sympathize with Olga's attempts to draw up the repressed idea from the unconscious.

Erlanger (in German, one who reaches out, attains) is one of Klamm's chief secretaries. The god of dreams, he is important to Klamm, the god of sexuality. In dreams one reaches the libidinous unconscious. Erlanger is 'famous for his splendid memory and his knowledge of people, he just draws his brows together and that's enough for him to recognize anybody, often people that he's never seen before, that he's only heard of or read about. . .' Recognition of people hitherto unseen is achieved easily in dreams by the processes of dream dynamics. Aptly enough, Erlanger leaves for the castle at five in the morning, after his night's work in the village. 'K. was struck by the fact that, though their discontent was general, nobody saw any objection to Erlanger's summoning his clients in the middle of the night. He asked why this was so and got the answer that they should be only too thankful to Erlanger. . .' He is told that in Erlanger's timetable there is no time allowed for journeys to the village. K. objects that even Klamm comes to the village by day. Is Erlanger more indispensable in the castle? 'One or two laughed good-humoredly, others maintained an embarrassed silence, the latter gained the ascendancy, and K. received hardly a reply. Only one man replied hesitatingly, that of course Klamm was indispensable, in the Castle as in the village.' The embarrassed silence is due not only to K.'s ignorance but also to the question of erotism involved in mentioning Klamm.

In seeking Erlanger K. meets a man named Bürgel (little castle). The god of sleep, he is one of the chief portals to the unconscious. He is an underling of Erlanger's. His face has childlike cheeks and eyes and an intellectual forehead, nose,

[136]

and mouth. As sleep he is both childlike and, through dreams, intelligent. There is no chair or table in his room, only a wide bed. He says that he had to choose between a narrow hotel bed with a complete set of furniture, and a wide bed and only a washstand, and that he chose the latter. 'Isn't the bed the main thing in the bedroom?' he asks. He speaks of the joys of sleep. He is a liaison secretary, the strongest link between Friedrich and the village. Slowly he lulls K. to sleep while chatting about night-hearings. He implies that a client always has a hidden opportunity of breaking down the castle gentlemen. In sleep one can draw close to the unconscious and perhaps obtain valuable clues to aid one in one's neurotic struggle. K. naps and dreams of victory. He dreams that he is battling a naked official who resembles a Greek god. He upsets the official's equanimity by sudden unexpected thrusts. He awakes, 'nauseated like an infant when it is awakened,' and thinks of Bürgel as the god. Finally, after more of Bürgel's chatter, he falls into a deep sleep.

3. THE OEDIPUS COMPLEX
The assistants.

The assistants symbolize K.'s deficient sexuality. They are not his real assistants. They are not permanently attached to the castle, but to the village. But, as temporary servants of the castle, they assume the infantilism and irrationality of the unconscious. They flourish while in castle service because of the castle's libidinous energy, and languish after they are dismissed by K.

'You're a difficult problem,' says K. to his assistants. 'How am I to know one of you from the other? The only difference between you is your names, otherwise you're as like as . . .' He stops, then continues involuntarily, 'You're as like as two snakes.' He might have said 'as like as two eggs,' which in colloquial German would have been an obvious sexual jest.

Instead, he disguises his thought by referring to the snake, a classic male symbol.

The cohabitation scene in the Herrenhof bar ends on a comic note. 'There on the bar counter sat his two assistants, a little heavy-eyed for lack of sleep, but cheerful. It was a cheerfulness arising from a sense of duty well done.' They have done their duty because K. has had a successful coitus. 'What are you doing here?' cries K., 'as if they were to blame for everything,' regretting his coitus with Frieda and blaming the assistants. 'It's in the daytime I need you, not in the night,' he says irritably and foolishly.

After the meeting with Momus, K. meets his assistants and cannot understand why he is disappointed to recognize them. The reason is that he has been hoping that he is on the way to the unconscious. He understands intuitively that the assistants are parodies of the unconscious.

K. learns from Jeremiah that Frieda has left him and that Arthur has gone to the castle to complain against him. Arthur (noble, lofty) is described by Jeremiah as a gentle sensitive soul. When K. asks Jeremiah why he wasn't frank about the nature of his duties Jeremiah responds, 'Because I was in the service, surely that's obvious,' indicating that he is an idea of the preconscious to whom an impulse from the unconscious had been temporarily attached. As a servant of the unconscious there was no question of frankness for him. Divorced from his job as K.'s assistant, he has lost the *élan* of the unconscious and is older in appearance. Besides, without Arthur he is without the pair relationship and therefore heterosexual and more mature. 'It's because I'm by myself. When I'm by myself then all my youthful spirits are gone,' he explains.

A humorous note is the revelation that the official Galater, deputizing for Klamm at the time, conferred the assistants upon K. with the order to cheer him up. Galater was the official who was saved from a fire by Olga's father. Galater was

[138]

therefore returning a favor when he conferred the assistants upon K.—an act of beneficence, since he knew that the Barnabas family were pinning their hopes on the land surveyor.

Frieda.

An Oedipus type is sexually inadequate. Relations with women are unpleasant if not impossible because of the incest guilt they engender. K., an Oedipus, loses Frieda because he discontinues coitus with her. Symbolically he achieves this by dismissing the assistants. Frieda resents him and supplants him with Jeremiah. When she is with K. she languishes, when back in the Herrenhof bar she blooms.

K.'s only successful coitus during the action of the novel occurs in his first encounter with Frieda, in the partial unconscious of the Herrenhof bar. His lack of sexual potency is obvious from his weakened condition afterwards. He lies abed 'the whole day through, and the whole night,' whereas Frieda, unaffected, tends him. His second coitus, accomplished in the Bridge Inn away from the unconscious, lacks an orgasm. Again Frieda is the aggressor. She clings to K. and they fall over on the bed.

There they lay, but not in the forgetfulness of the previous night. She was seeking and he was seeking, they raged and contorted their faces and bored their heads into each other's bosoms in the urgency of seeking something, and their embraces and their tossing limbs did not avail to make them forget, but only reminded them of what they sought; like dogs desperately tearing up the ground they tore at each other's bodies, and often, helplessly baffled, in a final effort to attain happiness they nuzzled and tongued each other's faces. Sheer weariness stilled them at last and brought them gratitude to each other.

An aspect of K.'s sexual difficulty is his inability to let himself go, to reach down into the sensual. He must always be master

[139]

of himself, always thoroughly conscious. Yet the sensual lures him, its enchantment is such 'that one could only go on and lose oneself further.' It is the enchantment of hell.

It comes to him not as a shock but as 'a faint glimmer of comfort' when Klamm's voice, the voice of parental authority, startles him in the act of coitus. Frieda revolts against the paternal majesty. K. thinks: 'What had happened? Where were his hopes?' He tells her they are both ruined. He feels guilty toward Klamm, feels he must elicit Klamm's pardon, also his permission to marry Frieda. He is an Oedipus, Frieda a Jocasta. Frieda is also Klamm's 'daughter.' Her revolt is anti-paternal. That she regards him as a father is clear from the fact that she calls the Bridge Inn landlady 'mother'; the latter is her 'mother' because she was Klamm's mistress before her.

K. tries to persuade Frieda that the assistants ought to be dismissed. Understanding that he wishes to dismiss coitus, she resists. He himself understands his meaning only uncon-sciously. Frieda pleads for them. Embarrassed—'She pressed closer to K. and hid her face on his shoulder'—she whispers faintly that she knows no way of dealing with them, adding that it will be impossible to discharge them. But she agrees to try. They retire for the night. K., awakened by a noise, finds one of the assistants lying beside him and 'this gave him the greatest fright that he had ever had since he first came to the village'—a reference to his fear of complete narcissism, ending in schizophrenia. He strikes the assistant. Frieda has been disturbed by some animal prowling about. As she returns to her place she strokes the weeping assistant sympathetically.

Next morning K. is punished by the two teachers for his aggression toward Frieda in depriving her of coitus. He is clawed by the cat and dismissed from his janitor's post. 'Look, that's what a sly, wicked cat has done to me,' he says, showing his bloody hand. He is secretly referring to the fact that the cat (symbol of animal passion) has injured him by arousing

Frieda's sensuality during the night—the cat crawled over her breast and awoke her. The caustic Gisa (in German *gis* means G-sharp) is responsible for the clawing. K.'s breaking into the woodshed (♀) and burning wood (♀), the reasons for his dismissal, are symbols of his injury to Frieda. Frieda resents him, therefore she 'sacrifices him to the assistants' by agreeing with them that K. broke the woodshed door. K. discharges the assistants, then notices how Frieda has changed.

It had been her unfailing liveliness and decision that had given her insignificant physique its beauty; now that beauty was gone. A few days of living with K. had been enough to achieve this. . . Or was her separation from Klamm the real cause of her falling away? It was the nearness of Klamm that had made her so irrationally seductive; that was the seduction which had drawn K. to her, and now she was withering in his arms.

Frieda mentions the resemblance between the assistants and Klamm, and warns K. that if he keeps hardening his heart to them he will never reach Klamm. 'In that case my only wish is for you to let them in. In that case let them in now at once. Don't bother about me; what do I matter? I'll defend myself as long as I can, but if I have to surrender, then I'll surrender with the consciousness that that too is for your sake.' But K., lost in the bleached wilds of the cerebral, cannot understand her. 'Never will they come in with my will,' he says.

There follow K.'s long conversation with Hans Brunswick and another with Frieda. His conversation with Hans is sly and full of overtones. Hans is a portrait of K., just as Hans the landlord is (the repetition of the names is not coincidental). Like K. he wishes to possess his mother. He has a sister named Frieda. K.'s Frieda is in a sense K.'s sister, since both have the same 'father' in Klamm. K. goes to find Barnabas at the latter's house, thinking of Schwarzer (in German, one who blackens) and of how Schwarzer is responsible for much of his trouble.

It is the knowledge that K. is attached to the Barnabas

family, to inversion, which convinced Frieda that she must give him up. She supplants him with Jeremiah, a childhood friend, who finds her 'respectable in any case' because she is a former sweetheart of Klamm, i.e. heterosexual. Frieda returns to her status in the Herrenhof bar, and as a result of this renewed contact with the unconscious she changes in appearance once again. K. attempts to win her back. Their argument is elaborated on two planes, K. speaking cerebrally and Frieda intuitively. By now Frieda despises K.'s cerebral obsession and accuses him of having never shown interest in her past (the emotional and poetic sides of her). She ends by saying that he can disprove everything, 'but in the end nothing is disproved.'

The Bridge Inn landlady.
Gardana strives to keep K. from reaching Klamm—both because she is a censor and because she was once Klamm's mistress. Gardana wishes to defend the 'father' against the aggression of the 'son.' Her efforts to protect Frieda from K. stem from her fear of irregularity.

Gardana strives to impress K. with his sexual inferiority by relating her experiences with Klamm, and she tempts him sexually to determine his potency, receiving him in bed and exhibiting sexual symbols, the three keepsakes she received from Klamm. She deplores Frieda's wasting herself on K.'s impotence after having been the mistress of a real man like Klamm, whom she compares to an eagle while comparing K. to a snake in the grass. She realizes that Frieda is moving toward neurosis, toward short-circuiting herself. Like Frieda, she is involved in an Oedipus situation. She mothers her husband, whom K. regards as a child. Her marriage has not been satisfactory because of her mother-son relationship with Hans. She has expended her pent-up passion in furious work and

[142]

has injured her health. She once calls her husband Martin (martial), afterwards always Hans (God is gracious). This is a deliberate Freudian slip; Gardana would like her husband to be 'martial.'

K. is neither convinced of Klamm's inaccessibility nor lured to approach Gardana sexually. Her attitude toward him stiffens and she soon orders him out of the house. She complains to Frieda that his behavior offends the honor of Klamm's keepsakes. It is his sexual irregularity that offends their honor.

'You are not from the Castle, you are not from the village, you aren't anything,' she once offers K. Her main objection to K. is his incestuous tendency, which involves the possibility of the dreaded homosexuality. Both she and Frieda fly at K. when he asserts that he can always find a bed to sleep in at Barnabas's. She threatens to expel him from her inn if he sleeps in the Barnabas house.

The Barnabas Family.

Amalia is a sexual invert. She suffers from a mother fixation. Inversion is one of the factors in an Oedipus fixation. K. is a partial invert. The figure of Amalia is a warning of the pit that lurks for K. when he denies the majesty of the castle. Barnabas too is a partial invert. Olga is the healthiest member of the family. She is also less neurotic than Frieda.

The title of the first subsection of Chapter xv is 'Amalia's Secret.' There is no secret on the surface. It exists only in the subterranean symbolism. The title is a hint of the existence of the symbolism. Amalia is connected in the story with a Sortini, K. with a Sordini. The similarity of names reveals the similarity between Amalia and K., the two inverts. Suffering from a mother fixation, Amalia has incestuous leanings toward her father. It was her incestuous desire that led her to reject the father imago, Sortini, with such violence. Her homosexual drives are so powerful that she exhausts herself in repressing

[143]

them (her name means industrious). She represents the pit that lurks for K. on the road to heterosexual salvation—the narcissistic pit of the Oedipus complex.

The Barnabas family is ostracized because Amalia rejects the heterosexual advances of a father image. In the village mythology the father is not capable of evil. Amalia is therefore regarded as malicious in denying Sortini's request on moral grounds. Whereas it is taboo for a son (K.) to seek incest with his mother (the castle), it is permissible for the father (Klamm, Sortini) to indulge in incest with his daughter (Frieda, Amalia, the landlady). This is a reflection of the dominance of males in the society that bred Kafka. Amalia's punishment clearly emanates from the castle, the unconscious. As Olga carefully points out: 'Nobody ought to be blamed, nobody could have done anything else, all that was already due to the influence of the Castle.' The family shares in the punishment because it helped create Amalia. The family's punishment would have been waived by the village if it had only behaved innocently, regardless of guilt. But, short-circuited between unconscious guilt and conscious innocence, it waited in bewilderment for a sign from Amalia, which the latter, in conflict herself, could not give.

Amalia's antagonism toward K. is explained by the difference in their sexual make-up. She is either irritated or indifferent in her relations with heterosexuals. She, the sexual extremist, disdains the sexual middle-man, caught between heterosexuality and inversion but moving toward the former. She accuses K. and Olga of castle gossip. K. asserts that 'people who don't care for such gossip and leave it all to others don't interest me particularly.' Amalia tells him of a young man who thought of nothing but the castle day and night, until it was feared he would lose his reason; it turned out the man was not thinking of the castle but of the daughter of a charwoman there; he married the girl. 'I think I would like that man,' says K. 'As for your liking the man, I doubt it,' retorts Amalia. 'It's probably his wife you would like.' She does not mean that K. is a philanderer but rather that he prefers women to men—that he is not a thorough invert like herself. Indications of Amalia's lack of normal interest are found in her ignorance of Frieda's name and of the fact that K. is engaged to Frieda. It was a clever stroke on Kafka's part to make the figure of the invert a female. A male invert would be obvious and might easily give away the entire psycho-analytic key.

Barnabas (consoling son) is a partial invert. Olga says, 'He has something of Amalia in him. And I'm sure that he doesn't tell me everything, although I'm his sole confidant.' Because of his taint of inversion, Barnabas makes no progress with the castle and he hinders K.'s relations with it.

It is a trick of Kafka's taken from the dynamics of censorship in dreams to disguise something by its opposite. He represents the depths of the unconscious by the castle hill. Emphasis on Olga's father is another example of the use of opposites, for it is her mother upon whom Amalia has fixated and toward whom her clandestine aggression is directed. The mother, mentioned only briefly, is in a worse state than her father. Olga says, '. . . and yet things are perhaps better with him than with my mother, for we're waiting daily for her death; it has been put off thanks to Amalia's superhuman efforts.' This innocent remark is significant inasmuch as un-consciously Amalia is actually prolonging the torment of her parents' lives, her oversolicitousness masking her sadism. The old couple, as well as Barnabas, are human sacrifices. The latter, meant by Olga to replace Sortini's messenger, has under-gone a striking change: as he probed the unconscious he aged and lost his daring and innocence.

Olga means more to K. than he comprehends: she is the least neurotic eligible woman in the village and for this reason is the most suitable as a mate for him. Her name means holy. She is portrayed as 'fresh and glowing from the frosty air, strong and vivid, as if transformed by the change from her usual aimless standing about inside.' A healthy extrovert who flourishes outside the house away from Amalia's domination, she is frank and simple, not sly and bitter like Amalia. And she is without Amalia's masculinity and biting comments concerning heterosexual persons. She is free of jealousy and therefore of any claim upon K. Her eyes are 'not cajoling, nor hectoring, but shyly simple and frank.' K. compares her favorably with Frieda (peace, the peace K. is seeking in heterosexuality), who is demanding, neurotic, and troublesome.

The landlady accepted a castle official whole-heartedly, Frieda half-heartedly, and Amalia rejected one altogether. A woman chosen by an official is doomed to unrest. But unrest is preferable to the ostracism consequent upon refusal of an official's advances. A healthy girl like Olga, capable of real object libido, is never summoned by a castle gentleman. Olga justifiably compares the relations between Frieda and Klamm to those between Amalia and Sortini. K., however, rebels. Understanding that his salvation lies in heterosexuality, it pains him to be connected with Amalia through Frieda. Olga says, penetratingly, 'The relation existing between the woman and the officials, believe me, is very difficult, or rather very easy to determine. Love always enters into it.' Love does enter in—in the form of libido—whether or not the official is accepted. Amalia's rejection of Sortini results from her incestuous love of her father. Olga adds rightly, 'But when all that's taken into account, what difference is left between Frieda and Amalia? One thing only, that Frieda did what Amalia refused to do.' K. replies that 'every attack on Frieda is an attack on myself'—i.e. on his heterosexuality. He insists that Frieda in her innocence has achieved more than Amalia in her pride. He speaks on one level of meaning while Olga speaks on another. Thus Kafka manages to achieve the effect of incompatibility of points of view.

Klamm.
    Klamm (in German, clammy) is the great father imago in The Castle. *He is described as a plump bourgeois, i.e. as similar to Kafka's father. On the surface he is seen as supremely virile and majestic. Secretly he is visualized as a phallus, since he is the male god of sex.*
    Olga says:

For he's reported as having one appearance when he comes into the village and another on leaving it, after having his beer he looks different from what he does before it, when he's awake he's different from when he's asleep, when he's alone he's different from when he's talking to people, and—what is comprehensible after all that—he's almost another person up in the Castle. And even within the village there are considerable differences in the accounts given of him, differences as to his height, his bearing, his size and the cut of his beard, fortunately there's one thing in which all the accounts agree, he always wears the same clothes, a black morning coat with long tails.

    Barnabas's difficulty in recognizing one male organ among many at the castle is a wild joke on Kafka's part; but even wilder is the manner in which Klamm receives Barnabas. 'He's usually admitted into a large room, but the room isn't even Klamm's bureau, nor even the bureau of any particular official.' This public room is the men's room. 'It's a room divided into two by a single reading-desk stretching all its length from wall to wall; one side is so narrow that two people can hardly squeeze past each other, and that's where clients wait, spectators, servants, messengers.' 'On the desk are great books lying open, side by side, and officials stand by most of them reading.' The books are the individual urinals. The 'reading' of the officials has an undeniably fluid character. The officials seem to be restless at this occupation.

They don't always stick to the same book, yet it isn't the books that they change but their places, and it always astounds Barnabas to see how they have to squeeze past each other when they change places, because there's so little room. In front of the desk and close to it there are small low tables at which clerks sit ready to write from dictation, whenever the officials wish it.

4. NOMENCLATURE

Gerstäcker alludes to the German author of the nineteenth century who was greatly influenced by the vogue of James Fenimore Cooper and whose passion was America. Kafka too wrote about America in the novel by that name. An autobiographical symbol is Gerstäcker's violent coughing, a reference to Kafka's tuberculosis. Another is the name Joseph, which K. gives to the castle functionary over the telephone when he pretends to be the land surveyor's old assistant. It alludes to the hero of *The Trial* and thereby to the novel itself. The date of the fire brigade festival, 3 July, is still another, being Kafka's birthday.

Yet another level of meaning is suggested by the trio of names, Count West-west, Gerstäcker, and Pinzgauer. We are here concerned with the myth of the life and death of the hero, with the hero's quest for rebirth, and with the conception of rebirth as a return to the womb—themes treated by Jung, who regarded Freud's Oedipus complex as merely one aspect of the quest for rebirth. Count West-west alludes to the west, where heroes die. One recalls that the sun, the prime father and hero symbol, dies in the west. The expression 'gone west' denotes someone who has died. Gerstäcker, alluding to America, is another reference to the west. Pinz-

The most interesting pattern of names is the Biblical trio: Jeremiah, Barnabas, and Galater, a combination that probably had spiritual and even philosophical significance for Kafka. Jeremiah represents the Old Testament and the Hebrews, Barnabas the New Testament and the Christians, Galater (in German, Galatians) the religious transition. Jeremiah was an exceptional, mystical Jew. He was not popular in his time because he castigated its corruption. His religion was more personal than the time allowed; he was for spirit as against form in religious practice. His laments were composed as the result of his bitterness. Kafka selected him to represent the Hebrews precisely because he was an exceptional Jew. The Biblical Barnabas was Paul's companion on his first missionary journey. Kafka's Barnabas is K.'s companion on the journey to the castle, which too is of a missionary nature, an effort to reform K.'s libido. The Galatians were Jews who were apostates to Christianity. They backslid, lured from the mysticism of the early Christians back to the Mosaic Code and the doctrine of historical revelation. They were the occasion for one of St. Paul's most famous epistles.

In the Hebrew and Christian traditions one finds the foundation of much of Western civilization. Both traditions gave rise to the Bible, which has been called the world myth. Kafka therefore gave himself the benefit of wide-ranging allusions when he selected representatives of both these traditions. And he presented his favorite contrast, form against spirit: the weighty cerebral tradition of the Hebrews against the mystical spirit of the early Christians.

The Jew, Saul of Tarsus, experienced both of these psychological and cultural phases. He applauded pogroms against the Christians, and later, through a mystical experience, he was converted to Christianity. As Paul he became one of the most important missionaries of the Gentile world. K. is Saul before he is reborn on the road to Damascus. Like

Saul he can be reborn only by accepting the unconscious, not by rejecting it. Therefore it may be said that Kafka viewed the overcerebration of the Hebrews as a neurotic symptom similar to his own and K.'s. The conflict between the Hebrews and the early Christians may be seen as an ancient form of the modern conflict between classicism and romanticism. Thus we have arrived, by a circuitous route, to our early thesis—that Kafka's works are attacks on cabalas.

vii

The Secret Meaning of *The Trial;* the Minor Writings

FOREWARNED by our insight into the cryptic content of *The Castle,* we approach *The Trial* with justified suspicion. Again we find that the tenets of psychoanalysis are carefully exploited. Joseph K.'s arrest is a symbolic one. It is not caused by a civil authority. He is not incarcerated. It is a psychic arrestation, a fixation classical in neurosis. He is arrested on the anal level of sexual development. And he is the victim of a castration complex.

My findings are fourfold:

1. *The Trial* contains a web of mythical symbolism.

2. It is a literary panorama of the states of consciousness as discovered by the psychoanalytic movement.

3. It presents in detail the dynamics of the castration complex.

4. It contains nomenclatural symbolism.

1. SYMBOLISM

There are two types of symbolism in The Trial: *mythical symbolism and symbolic action.*

Mythical symbolism. A bank is a repository for money. Money is a symbol of ordure. Therefore K.'s bank has an anal character. The black coat the warders insist he wear symbolizes his coming death. K. himself understands its symbolism better than he realizes when he says, 'But this isn't the capital charge yet.' The inspector's advice, '. . . think less about us and more of what is to happen to you, think more about yourself instead,' is seen to be psychoanalytically sound. K.'s desire to call Hasterer, the public prosecutor, indicates his civil orientation regarding his case.

Mythical symbols are prominent in Chapter 1. The pleats, pockets, buttons, and belt of the first warder are all sexual symbols. Others are nightshirt, underwear, thirtieth birthday (use of the trinity), dipping bread and butter into the honey pot, pincushion, grouping objects around the candle, uniforms, the inspector and two warders (three), the three young men, the three spectators, the inspector's 'hard round hat,' which he places carefully on his head, 'as if he were trying it on for the first time,' K.'s hat, et cetera.

K.'s infantilism is suggested by a social symbol, Frau Grubach's apron string, at which he glances down 'as so often before.' Frau Grubach is a mother image. She herself says to K., 'It's a matter of your happiness, and I really have that at heart, more perhaps than I should, for I am only your landlady.' The fact that K. seems unclean is emphasized by the triple (♂) refusal of his hand—first by the inspector, second by the three clerks, and third by Frau Grubach—and by K.'s mortification, also the embarrassment of those who refuse it.

In the second part of Chapter 1 female symbols are more in evidence than male, since this part is concerned with Fräulein Bürstner: stockings, moon, blouse, pillows, window, silk shawl, chink of the door, night table, chest.

In the description of the examining magistrate's notebook —'yellow-edged leaves'—we come upon the first of several instances of the use of the color yellow, which in dreams is generally found in a pre-phallic (i.e. anal) context.

K. visits the law-court offices in the garret. There he meets other 'accused' men. The hats (♂) of these receive attention. They are not on hatracks but under the benches. This seemingly innocent detail conceals a hint of sexual difficulties. The men are cowed, convinced of their worthlessness. Their humility provokes K.'s sadism. (Sadism and masochism are characteristic of the anal stage.) 'That ridiculous outcry was too much for K.; if the man would not believe that he was under arrest, so much the better; perhaps he actually took him for a Judge.' He flings one of the accused against a bench, thus rejecting even his own 'colleagues.' A warder runs up and K. gapes at his sword (♂) 'and actually put out his hand to feel it.' The warder seems to be suffering from gout (♂), like the superintendent of *The Castle*. K.'s infantilism is evidenced in the scene with the girl and the clerk of inquiries. Like a child, he grows panicky and ill and completely dependent because he is lost among the offices. The clerk, a father surrogate, enjoys K.'s terror. The girl, a mother image, explains apologetically, as if out of guilt, afraid that the clerk's laughter was insulting.

In Chapter IV there are sun (♂), moon (♀), Montag's limp (♂), the long narrow dining-room (♀), the three (♂) chairs in Fräulein Bürstner's room. In Chapter V there are lumber (♀), room (♀), ink bottles (♀), three (♂) men, candle (♂), moon (♀), hand barrows (♀). In Chapter VIII there are candle (♂), the number three (♂), pen (♂) and inkwell (♀), candle drippings. The number five is prominent here (Block's case is over five years old and he has five advocates besides Huld). This number appears unobtrusively throughout the novel and it also appears on a few occasions in *The Castle*. It symbolizes the union of the sexes (3 plus 2). Odd numbers are traditionally masculine and even feminine. In the final chapter are hats (♂), the number three (♂), children (♂), bridge (♂), moonlight (♀), water (♀), knife

(♂), et cetera. Someone who is either Fräulein Bürstner or resembles her fails to help K. in his last moments. The mother fails to protect the son from the castrating father.

Symbolic action. K. makes much of the magistrate's question, 'You are a house painter?,' a seeming error, failing to recognize the possibility that the magistrate was striving to spare his feelings by avoiding a reference to his bank work. Although painting is a sublimated coprophilic urge, it does not have the immediate and obvious symbolism of bank.

K. proudly announces, 'I'm the junior manager of a large Bank.' His fantastic innocence causes the party of the right to laugh so heartily that K. laughs too. K.'s laughter arises from his unconscious awareness of his ridiculousness and of the symbolism of his occupation. The laughter is great: 'People doubled up with their hands on their knees and shook as if in spasms of coughing. There were even a few guffaws from the gallery.'

K. is overbearing and boastful—'I do not say that your procedure is contemptible, but I should like to present that epithet to you for your private consideration.' He identifies himself with the great universal cause of freedom, although in reality he is concerned only with his own affair, as he admits later on several occasions. His behavior is infantile. He is disconcerted by the genital, which for all its vulgarity is more mature and manly than he is—once he is interrupted when the washerwoman enters the room and again when the student embraces her and screams.

K. is an exhibitionist. (Exhibitionism and voyeurism are features of the anal stage.) ' "I have no wish to shine as an orator," said K., having come to this conclusion, "nor could I if I wished." ' But he obviously enjoys his proud oratory. He condemns the proceedings as well as the details of his arrest. He presumes to interpret certain activities of the magistrate as evidence of collusion. Kafka presents evidence objectively, leaving the reader to judge. Instead of saying that the magistrate made a sign he says that K. 'thought he could see him catching someone's eye in the audience, as if giving him a sign'; instead of saying that the magistrate was embarrassed, he says, 'The Examining Magistrate kept fidgeting on his chair with embarrassment or impatience.' He adds: 'The man behind him to whom he had been talking bent over him again, either to encourage him or to give him some particular counsel.'

In Chapter iv, 'Fräulein Bürstner's Friend,' K. suffers a serious reversal. It is he who is rejected, not he who rejects, although at the very end of the chapter he petulantly rejects Lanz, Montag, and Bürstner. Bürstner avoids him and shields herself by means of Montag. Montag means Monday, the day of the moon, and moon alludes to chastity, virginity, menses, and madness (moonstruck, lunacy). Thus Bürstner protects herself by means of her monthly affliction (her friend tells K. that Bürstner 'is feeling a little unwell today'), by Montag's queerness (she trails about and forgets her underwear), and by means of a roommate who will act as chaperon. That she herself is not virginal is indicated by Frau Grubach's remarks concerning her relations with men. But she will have nothing to do with K. because he is sexually an infant. She understands that he wishes to discuss his 'case' with her, that he desires her aid, that he unknowingly wants to attain to full sexual maturity; but she is soured on him because of the scene in her room. Her selection of Montag to defend her is shrewd, for she presents to K. a portrait of woman as unclean and crazy. When K. refuses to finish his breakfast, crying, 'Oh, take it away, all the same' at Grubach, it seems to him 'as if Fräulein Montag were mixed up with everything, it was too sickening.' This brief chapter brilliantly summarizes both K.'s difficulties with women as well as their rejection of him.

The cathedral, like the castle, is a mother symbol (cf. Mother Church). K. is assigned to escort an Italian visitor on a tour. The Italian seems to be fixated like K. He too is a connoisseur of 'art treasures and monuments' and probably, like K., is a member of a society for the preservation of ancient monuments—i.e. monuments of one's infancy. He makes a sexual dig at K., saying 'laughingly that someone was an early riser from the bed,' an allusion to K.'s insufficiency. He never appears at the cathedral. His function is to lure K. there. He is an agent of the court. That he belongs to the unconscious is evidenced by his unintelligibility to K. and by his irrationality and vigor. The scoptophiliac factor is involved, since K. is to take him on a sight-seeing tour.

Leni calls K. at the bank, learns he must go to the cathedral and says, 'They're driving you hard.' She understands the significance of his summons to the cathedral and even he, who does not grasp its symbolism consciously, has an intuition of its meaning, for he answers, 'half to himself and half to the far-away girl who could no longer hear him: "Yes, they're driving me hard." ' Leni's call is an impulse from the unconscious that reaches his conscious mind.

The summons to the cathedral is a summons to symbolic, spiritual death. Going to the cathedral is symbolic of the return to the womb, of death in the process of rebirth. K. has unconsciously been longing for death and the hope of rebirth. He has taken to staring out of his office window (♀). The weather has turned slushy and snowy—water is a symbol of rebirth. The cathedral square is deserted and the window-blinds of the houses around it are drawn because the cathedral is a place of death. It is very dark inside, the approaching gloom of extinction and the womb.

The cathedral is a function of the court, not vice versa. It is the court that represents the unconscious. The cathedral-as-mother is not the unconscious itself, as the castle is, but rather a subsidiary symbol. If it were the prime symbol it would not be relegated to one chapter. Hence the symbolic

[158]

use of cathedral is not to be taken as Kafka's underwriting a benevolent religion. On the contrary: the cathedral is used to suggest a place of darkness and doom, and the priest, as father image, offers K. castration threats. The cathedral is a device of the court. Read psychoanalytically, this means that religion is a function of the unconscious. K., then, is on the way to rebirth. It is in this context that his first name is most meaningful: the Joseph of Old Testament fame was twice cast into the pit and each time was reborn. Ironically, Kafka's real name, Franz, means free, therefore he could not use it, although he was able to employ his final initial.

The priest calls K.'s name and announces that he is the prison chaplain. Speaking for the unconscious, he says, 'The verdict is not so suddenly arrived at, the proceedings only gradually merge into the verdict.' He tells K., 'You cast about too much for outside help, especially from women. Don't you see that it isn't the right kind of help?' He relates the legend of the doorkeeper. Freud himself once created a similar legend: he said that the censor between the conscious and the unconscious is like a doorkeeper keeping out certain mental excitations. The doorkeeper in Kafka's legend is this same Freudian censor guarding the entrance to the law, the unconscious. The man from the country is K. himself, too timid and too neurotic to demand admittance. From this context it is seen that the doorkeeper did not delude the man, inasmuch as it was his function to act as censor. The man deluded himself —or rather his neurosis deluded him.

2. THE DEPTH PSYCHOLOGY

The bank symbolizes the conscious mind, the boarding-house the preconscious (Grubach, the landlady's name, seems to be derived from the German grube, pit, cavity, underground), and the court the unconscious. The boardinghouse, like the preconscious, is the basis of morality, normality, con-

science and fecundity. It contains Montag, the teacher, symbol of conscience and morality. The court, like the unconscious, is primitive, irrational, infantile, and amoral.

The warders, representing the unconscious, announce K.'s psychic arrest. They are minor officials of the unconscious and do not presume to understand the profounder motives of the organization's behavior. One of them says: 'Our officials, so far as I know them, and I know only the lowest grades among them, never go hunting for crime in the populace, but, as the Law decrees, are drawn towards the guilty and must then send out us warders. That is the Law. How could there be a mistake in that?' Guilt, in short, is internal, and ignorance of this law is no ground for defense. Whether one is aware of the unconscious or not, it has its influence on one's health.

Joseph K. is informed by telephone that 'next Sunday a short inquiry into his case would take place.' It is noteworthy that he hears from the court *via* telephone, for the aural sense seems to be typical of the unconscious in this novel. The telephone also has phallic value, as in *The Castle*. Sunday is the day apart from the conscious week at the bank, and is therefore preferred by the unconscious. The court holds out the possibility of night hearings, suggesting the connection between the unconscious and night. Its location is among the poor, the 'lower' class, the lower depths, a topographic characterization. From this stem all the details of poverty, tenements, dust, and chaos used to describe the court.

The sexual significance of K.'s case is highlighted by the introduction of the three (♂) bank clerks during K.'s first visit to the court. The visual element is emphasized: K. catches sight of them, and Kaminer bends inquisitively over the railing at K. The house in which the interrogation will take place is located on Juliusstrasse or Julius Street. Julius means downy-bearded. It is an allusion to the immature nature of the unconscious. The motif of children is prominent in the descriptions

[160]

of the neighborhood. Also prominent is the aural sense: people shout to each other across the street, laugh loudly, a vendor cries his wares and a phonograph begins 'stridently to murder a tune.' What is aural for K. is oral to someone else, usually some member of the unconscious. The oral stage is the earliest, according to psychoanalysis. The people of the unconscious are characterized as infantile by the use of oral symbols. Another aspect of this symbolism is K.'s infantile fear of loud sounds.

As in *The Castle*, the depth of the unconscious is represented by its opposite, height: the courts are located high in a tenement. As K. seeks the interrogation room he comes upon three (♂) other flights of stairs, as well as a young girl in her night jacket, standing at a pump (♂) while the water pours into her bucket (♀). When K. comes upon the children playing marbles and they glare at him, he thinks: 'If I ever come here again I must either bring sweets to cajole them with or else a stick to beat them,' a thought that typifies his extremism, infantilism, and sadism. He invents a joiner named Lanz because Lanz implies lance (♂), from the German *lanze,* and is therefore a good password to the libidinous unconscious. K. sees in the inquiry room the great pendulum clock, a symbol of both the male and female organs. He is led to the examining magistrate by 'a little red-cheeked lad,' a further indication of the infantilism of the unconscious.

In *The Castle* the unconscious is passive, in *The Trial* it is aggressive. The examining magistrate says to K., 'You should have been here an hour and five minutes ago,' setting the tone of the proceedings. The unconscious, the court, is peopled by men. Joseph K.'s efforts to reach the highest court are analogous to K.'s efforts to reach the castle, in that he wishes to reach his unconscious—the source of his neurosis—and his mother. But the incestuous implications of *The Castle* are for the most part indirect in *The Trial*. Joseph K. desires his mother as protection against his father's castration threats. Partly convinced of his castration, he identifies himself with her, who also lacks the male organ. He is not simply an anal type; he is an anal type suffering from a castration complex. Freud has sharply emphasized the intimate connection between the anal phase and the castration complex, as well as between the castration and Oedipus complexes. The battle with the fathers is a struggle to preserve K.'s masculinity.

The unconscious is amoral. The washerwoman accepts adultery as a matter of course, saying, 'I stand excused in the eyes of everyone who knows me.' She exists on the fringes of the unconscious. She has a penetrating insight into K., she understands that his defiance is harmful to him. 'It didn't do you any harm to have your speech interrupted; what you said made a bad enough impression to judge from the discussion afterwards.' She is inconsistent: she disapproves of his speech, yet says she liked it; she is weary of his reforming zeal, yet unduly interested in it. Freud has shown that contradictory ideas and impulses exist simultaneously in the unconscious. She makes overtures to K. but he responds, characteristically, with non-erotic intentions, like K. of *The Castle* resisting sexuality and the unconscious.

3. THE CASTRATION COMPLEX
Joseph K.

Joseph K. is an early anal type, in contrast with Block, the late anal type. As an early anal type, he is a rejecter. Block, the late anal type, is a retainer.

It is by no means accidental that Joseph K. is accosted in bed and in a nightshirt, for he is arrested on an infantile level, a level of dependency. We see him, embarrassed, waiting for Anna to bring him his breakfast. But Anna (grace), never appears. 'Though it was not usual with him to learn from experience' is a revealing clause, underlining his fixated

[162]

state. 'You're behaving worse than a child,' cries the tall warder—another revealing statement. K. searches for his identification papers and is about to settle for his bicycle license (a bit of childish irrationality); he finally finds his birth certificate (a reference to infancy). The theme of K.'s infantilism is played upon ingeniously. His delight at having escaped a bath is a typical motif.

His most pressing problem is to progress from anal to genital eroticism. That is why the warders, symbolizing his virility, are important for him, although he does not recognize this. In the debates between him and the warders and inspector we are offered, as in *The Castle*, a verbal dramatization of the incompatibility between mental levels. The inspector and warders speak truthfully in their universe of discourse, for which K. possesses no key. What is true on the plane of social symbolism (in which the warders of *The Trial* and the landladies of *The Castle*, for example, are liars) is reversed on the subterranean level. As a result Kafka's work is shot through with paradox.

The magistrate's books prove to be indecent—at least that is what K. thinks. But he is still unaware that he is dealing with a libidinous court. The indecent picture in the first book is childishly drawn. The title of the second is meaningful: *How Grete Was Plagued by Her Husband Hans*. Grete (from Margaret) means pearl or child of light, Hans (from Johannes) means the Lord graciously giveth or Jehovah is gracious. The noble names suggest the nobility of the libido. The intention of the book is thus not obscene. But K., to whom the genital is repugnant, regards it as such.

The examining magistrate, a father image like Klamm, like the latter enjoys women. K.'s daydream of wresting the woman away from the magistrate contains incestual implications, since as the lover of the magistrate-father, the woman is a mother imago for K. The student is a father image and his beard, which he is always fingering, and bowed legs, are sexual symbols. He wins the woman from K. It is only after K. loses her that he regards her sexually. K.'s sadism is pictured by his thoughts of revenge and by his punching of the student's back.

Joseph K. is in search of his masculinity. The female symbols are mainly present to emphasize the male, just as the role of females is to arouse K.'s genital awareness. Bürstner's part is crucial. She lets K. down, even at the very end, just before his execution. (The name Bürstner seems to be derived from the German, *bürster*, brusher; it seems to fit her, as one who brushes K. aside.) Elsa is by contrast good to K., on an extrovertive plane (the name means noble maiden). But she is too regular to attract him deeply. Bürstner is, like Frieda, neurotic enough to make him wish to possess her. Both are probably modeled on F.B., hence their similarity.

Just as in *The Castle*, salvation depends on acceptance of the unconscious. But Joseph K., like K., is too cerebral to accept the irrational. Besides, he is a rejecter. He rejects the warders, the magistrates, the advocate, Leni, the bank. Block, the commercial traveler, 'retains' six advocates although only one is permitted. The name Rudi Block is amusing. Rudi (from Rudolf) means famous wolf, famous hero, famous ruler. Block implies stolidity. All this is applied satirically to the cringing Block.

K., with his pattern of rejection, needs objects to reject, therefore when he is not summoned to a second interrogation he goes of his own accord. This time his hostility turns inward, with striking results, leaving him as helpless as the infant he is.

The people around K. illuminate him brightly. Frau Grubach, the prime mother surrogate, is unhealthily devoted to him, weeping aloud when he is cross with her. Realizing that she is emotionally dependent on him, he is often brutal to her. His anal sadism is clearest in his treatment of her. He

[164]

crushes the sugar in the bottom of his cup as if he were symbolically crushing her. He lets no opportunity pass to tyrannize her.

Grubach, speaking of his arrest, says strikingly: 'It gives me the feeling of something very learned, forgive me if what I say is stupid, it gives me the feeling of something abstract which I don't understand, but which I don't need to understand.' What she says is far from stupid, referring as it does to the 'abstract' arrest of K.'s psyche. But K. sees his arrest only in cerebral terms, in terms of common civil arrests. In the bank, he says, he is always prepared; there he would not be caught napping. '. . . above all my mind is always on my work and so kept on the alert, it would be an actual pleasure to me if a situation like that cropped up in the Bank.'

K.'s inability to deal with Bürstner on a mature sexual level—even though she makes certain encouraging gestures, such as pressing her hips with her open palms, and behaving passively before his advances—is underscored by his exhibitionism (he acts out the scene of the inspector's interrogation and bawls out his name compulsively in childish imitation of the father-inspector), his masochism (he is willing to be charged with assaulting Bürstner), and by his abortive sexual gestures (he kisses her on the brow, then later first on the lips, 'then all over the face, like some thirsty animal lapping greedily at a spring of long-sought fresh water.'). She grows weary and depressed under such infantile ministrations and resigns her hand for him to kiss, 'half turning away as if she were unaware of what she did. . .'

Captain Lanz typifies the normal sexual male. 'His politeness towards Fräulein Montag was in striking contrast to the treatment which she had received from K.' K. sees Lanz, a father imago, as aiding Fräulein Montag to bar his way to Bürstner. The symbol of virility bars the pregenital neurotic's way to heterosexuality.

[165]

Montag significantly is a teacher. Besides, she teaches French, something foreign (just as woman is foreign to K.) and something with *risqué* associations (also foreign to K.).

The uncle learned of K.'s difficulties from his niece Erna (retiring), a shy girl who wrote him, 'After I had waited meekly for a while I asked an attendant if the interview was likely to last much longer.' She claims that K. sent her a big box of chocolates for her birthday and she emphasizes the theme of chocolates by adding, 'For I may tell you that chocolate vanishes on the spot in this boardinghouse, hardly do you realize that you've been presented with a box when it's gone.' The chocolates are a fecal motif and the theater tickets which K. resolves to send her regularly are, a reference to scoptophilia. The motif of theater occurs three (δ) times in the novel: Bürstner is said to be at the theater, K. resolves to send Erna theater tickets, and he asks his executioners what theater they are playing at.

The whipper and interrogation scenes.

Chapter v, 'The Whipper,' is a chapter of sadism, masochism, and castration symbols, graphically connecting the concepts of the anal type and the castration complex, and indicating how the consequences of K.'s 'arrest' can make themselves known in his conscious mind. In the dreams and fantasies of castration neurotics, whipping often symbolizes the act or the imminent threat of castration. Here the whipper is seen to apply the rod (δ) to the warders. The whipper is a father image. The anal context is indicated by the scoptophiliac emphasis: 'One of the men, who was clearly in authority over the two and took the eye first'; K. stares at the men, studies the switch, looks attentively at the whipper; 'and without glancing at the Whipper again—such things should be done with averted eyes on both sides—'; K. stares 'in the direction from which the clerks must presently come running';

he stares into the courtyard and in the street he carefully observes everyone he passes, looking for the warder's girl.

K.'s sadism (he throws Franz down) and his masochism (he considers substituting himself for the warders) are clearly emphasized. He is fascinated by windows. Their value is twofold: they are female symbols and they permit him to exercise his scoptophilia. The female element is heightened by a reference to the moon: 'but the topmost panes cast back a faint reflection of the moon.'

The repetition of the whipping scene on the following day symbolizes K.'s fixation. 'Everything was still the same, exactly as he had found it on opening the door the previous evening.' It is this state of fixation, this suspension in the pit of hell, that terrifies K.

In the interrogation scene it is the student, a male, who shrieks, not the washerwoman. The woman disturbs K. merely by her female presence, upsetting his pregenital posturing; but the student upsets him as do men, who are his father-persecutors. The orderly meeting develops into a gigantic castration threat. 'On the contrary they actually obstructed him, someone's hand—he had no time to turn round—seized him from behind by the collar, old men stretched out their arms to bar his way, and by this time K. was no longer thinking of the couple, it seemed to him as if his freedom were being threatened, as if he were being arrested in earnest, and he sprang recklessly down from the platform.' The beards of the fathers are 'stiff and brittle,' (♂) and dangerous—'to take hold of them would be like clutching bunches of claws rather than beards.' K. discovers that the right and left are really one party and makes his defiant exit.

Scoptophilia.
  Scoptophilia is an element of the anal stage. Joseph K. is a chronic voyeur.

[167]

The motif of scoptophilia dominates Chapter ɪ (from which the following references are taken). Thereafter it is a subordinate although still powerful motif.*

K. *watches* from his pillow the old lady opposite, 'who seemed to be *peering* at him with a curiosity unusual even for her. . .' He rings the bell and a man enters 'whom he had never *seen* before in the house.' There follows a description of the man, with an emphasis on visual details. The man's outfit *looks* eminently practical. After a short exchange Joseph K. *studies* the fellow with silent intensity. 'The man did not submit to this *scrutiny* for very long. . .' Joseph K. springs out of bed and cries: 'I must *see* what people these are next door. . .'

In the next room 'everything *looked* at first glance almost as it had done the evening before.' There is a visual description of the room. 'Through the open window he had another *glimpse* of the old woman, who with genuine senile inquisitiveness had moved along to the window exactly opposite, in order to *see* all that could be *seen*.' Kafka describes her as senile while emphasizing her voyeurism, a reference to the infantilism of senility. K.'s visual sense is so strong that it hypnotizes him. ' "I'd better get Frau Grubach—" said K., as if wrenching himself away from the two men (though they were standing at quite a distance from him) and making as if to go out.' It is emphasized by the tricks it plays on him. 'K. felt he must sit down, but now he saw that there was no seat in the whole room except the chair beside the window.' The two warders advance on him and overtop him enormously, then they *examine* his nightshirt, as if inspecting it for embarrassing

* The English translation by the Muirs is a faithful representation of the original text. The preponderance of scoptophiliac references cited here is also to be found in the German original. All of the italics in this context are mine.

stains. K. *catches sight* of the second warder's face, and the face is described.

He sees Grubach for an instant, *looks* at the door she has closed, and is recalled to attention by a shout from the warders. He *sees* them devouring his breakfast and asks them to *show* him their papers. 'Without wishing it Joseph K. found himself decoyed into an exchange of speaking *looks* with Franz. . .' Then 'he could still *see* the old woman, who had now dragged to the window an even older man, whom she was holding round the waist.' Eventually still another person will join the old woman, forming the male trinity. The function of these gazers is to emphasize the visual motif as well as to embarrass K., to make him feel exposed, as though he were somehow tainted.

'They were quite at liberty to *watch* him now. . .' Joseph K. is ordered to appear before the inspector. K. picks up a coat and *displays* it for the warders. He proceeds to Bürstner's room, the changes in which are described from the visual point of view. Three (♂) young men are *viewing* her *photographs*. (The use of photographs and paintings, emphasizing the visual motif, is extensive in *The Trial*.) The trio at the window *stares* at the proceedings. The inspector amuses himself by restless activity which appeals to K.'s eyes—'with both hands rearranging the few things that lay on the night-table, a candle and a matchbox, a book and a pincushion, as if they were objects which he required for his interrogation.' The inspector at one point *looks* to see how many matches there are in the matchbox.

K. *stares* at the inspector after the latter has rebuked him. Irritated, he shouts, 'Here's a fine crowd of *spectators!*' and points at the trio at the window. Now the inspector compares the length of his fingers, while the three young men *look* aimlessly about. K. suddenly learns that they are clerks from the bank, his eyes having deceived him till now. He *gapes* at them. The three are characterized by descriptions that are visual: 'The stiff Rabensteiner swinging his arms, the fair Kullich with the deep-set eyes, and Kaminer with his insupportable smile, caused by a chronic muscular twitch.'

K. *glances* down at Frau Grubach's apron string. On the way to the bank Kullich points out the opposite house door, 'where the tall man with the fair, pointed beard was emerging into *sight*. . .' 'Don't *look* across,' says K. hurriedly. He turns around and *cranes* from the back of the car to see if he can perhaps *catch sight* of the inspector and the warders. '. . . Rabensteiner *gazed* out to the right, Kullich to the left, and only Kaminer faced him. . .'

K. several times calls the three clerks at the bank 'with no other purpose than to *observe* them.' He finds a young lad at the doorway of the boardinghouse. ' "Who are you?" K. asked at once, bringing his face close to the lad's, one could not *see* very well in the darkness of the entrance.' He goes upstairs and turns around for another *look*. He *looks* around Frau Grubach's room and *gazes* at her 'with a certain gratitude.' K. *looked* on in silence while she took up her darning again. He asks her to shake his hand, '*gazing* at the woman with a different, a critical eye.' Frau Grubach announces that Bürstner's room is in order, inviting K. to *see* for himself. K. *looks* in. A little later K. lounges by the window and shuts his tired eyes while waiting for Bürstner. 'When he became weary of *gazing* out into the empty street he lay down on the sofa, after having slightly opened the door to the entrance hall, so that from where he was lying he might *see* at once anyone who came in.'

'He felt no special desire to *see* her, he could not even remember exactly how she *looked*. . .' When she appears K. *observes* her carefully. She herself '. . . cast a critical *eye* round the room instead of *looking* at him.' They *gaze* into each other's eyes. At one point he is 'completely taken up in staring' at Bürstner. He insists on *showing* her how the morning's interrogation occurred, in minute detail, asking her to *picture* to herself the arrangement of people. 'Fräulein Bürstner, silent and limp, *stared* at the floor. . . He was *gazing* at her hair. . . He expected her to *look* up at him. . .'

Auditory hyperesthesia.

The motif of the father-as-aural is powerful in The Trial. *Auditory hyperesthesia is prominent in the anal character.*

Whereas K. feels comfortable in the visual sphere the aural one disconcerts him, as if it were the voice of the father. Yet it attracts him too. The inspector's shout of command 'was actually welcome to him.' When K. himself breaks into shouting the warders instantly lower their voices, as if in respect for his sudden maturation.

The warders are presented aurally: 'A short guffaw from the next room came in answer; one could not tell from the sound whether it was produced by several individuals or by one.' The auditory motif is strong in the whipper chapter. K. hears convulsive sighs behind the lumber room door, the warders cry out to him for help and Franz shrieks with pain.

K.'s uncle, while not a creature of the unconscious, is largely a primitive type, a satire on the man of practical affairs. Like the clan of the unconscious, he impresses himself on K.'s auditory sense—crying out, spluttering, bellowing, ejaculating. He embarrasses K. with his loud talk, so that K. says, 'But you're talking too loudly, Uncle, I feel pretty certain the attendant is standing behind that door listening, and I dislike the idea.' At one point, when the uncle curses Leni, 'K. started up in alarm, though he had expected some such outburst, and rushed over to his uncle with the firm intention of clapping both hands over his mouth and so silencing him.' The uncle's raucous laughter before the chief clerk of the court at Huld's embarrasses K. so that he thinks, 'A hateful moment!' The uncle is thoroughly irrational and violent, also somewhat compulsive with his stuffing of papers underneath him without looking at them, his hurrying, shouting, and gesturing. He too is neurotic but he has adjusted by becoming aggressive.

In the first paragraph of Chapter VI the uncle is referred to as Uncle Karl, whereas in all other instances he is named Albert. Karl means a man; also, according to some authorities, it is analogous to Charles, which means strong and robust and also has the connotation of churl. These accurately characterize K.'s uncle. But it is Joseph K. who uses this name. The name Albert is used by the uncle himself, when he says to the advocate, 'It's your old friend Albert.' Albert means nobly bright. Nobly bright is unquestionably how the uncle fancies himself. Albert is his name, as the advocate affirms. The use of the name Karl is a deliberate Freudian slip used by Kafka as part of his dramatization of Freudian mechanics, and as a key to K.'s thinking concerning his uncle.

The auditory motif is prominent in the cathedral scene. The priest calls out K.'s name. At one point he shrieks. 'And at that the priest shrieked from the pulpit: "Can't you see anything at all?" It was an angry cry, but at the same time sounded like the involuntary shriek of one who sees another fall and is startled out of himself.'

The warders.

The warders, like K.'s assistants in The Castle, *symbolize Joseph K.'s testicles and his deficient sexuality. They are servants of the court. They possess the irrationality and infantilism of the unconscious.*

They proclaim themselves Joseph K.'s benefactors—they say that they probably mean better by him and stand closer to him than any other people in the world—and this is justified by their names, Franz (free) and Willem (protector, defender —from Wilhelm).

[172]

Huld.

Huld (in German, grace, favor, benevolence) symbolizes a psychoanalyst.

Huld is characterized as a 'poor man's lawyer,' an allusion to the symbolism of the unconscious as the 'lower' class. Huld's house is in 'the very suburb where the Law Court had its attic offices'; nevertheless he is not so poor as he makes out, for when K. goes with Leni into his office, he finds it 'a lofty, spacious room, the clients of this "poor man's" lawyer must feel lost in it. K. pictured to himself the timid, short steps with which they would advance to the huge table.' Huld's poverty is only symbolic, like the poverty of the court.

K. says, 'I don't know that in a case like this one can even employ an advocate,' but the uncle assures him one can. When K. relates his story to the uncle he leaves out 'no single detail,' yet he mentions Fräulein Bürstner's name 'only once and in passing . . . since Fräulein Bürstner had no connection with the case.' Thus K. is innocent of her real meaning.

K. is surprised that Huld is acquainted with his case. 'I'm an Advocate, you see,' says Huld, 'I move in circles where all the various cases are discussed, and the more striking ones are bound to stick in my mind.. . .' These circles may be psychoanalytical societies and/or literature, in which case-histories are prominent. K. does not grasp Huld's symbolism and is disturbed by his extra-legal status. ' "But you're attached to the Court in the Palace of Justice, not to the one with the skylight," he wanted to say, yet could not bring himself actually to say it.' The advocate does not need to attend the court to obtain his information. It is brought to him by patients and court functionaries (such as, perhaps, journals and professional correspondence). He claims that 'this intercourse benefits me in all sorts of ways, some of which won't even bear mentioning.' The chief clerk of the court is presented correctly as a creature of darkness, since he belongs to the unconscious.

[173]

The beginning of Chapter VII is an amusing satire on psychoanalysts and their methods. It does not necessarily represent Kafka's views, inasmuch as K.'s antagonism to Huld is part of his pattern of rejection. K. thinks that a written defense has undoubted advantages over the use of an advocate. He still believes he is dealing with some sort of civil court. He resents Huld because Huld hardly cross-examines him. 'And there were so many questions to put. To ask questions was surely the main thing. . . But the Advocate, instead of asking questions, either did all the talking or sat quite dumb opposite him. . .' This resentment of the seeming passivity of the analyst is typical of neurotic patients. 'Now and then he would give K. some empty admonitions such as people hand out to children.' The advocate speaks of other cases to K., a summary of which he has in his desk but which he cannot show him because it contains official secrets: a reference to the case-histories of other patients and to the doctor's inability to divulge professional matters. 'Nevertheless the vast experience he had gained through all these cases would now redound to K.'s benefit.'

K. is told that an accused man is permitted only one advocate—i.e. a patient is permitted only one analyst at a time. The private, indefinite, trial-and-error methods of psychoanalysis are indicated by Huld's remarks on the courts—how they sometimes mislay the first plea or hardly ever read it, how the proceedings are not public, how the legal records 'and above all the actual charge-sheets' are inaccessible to the accused and his counsel, how the defense is 'not actually countenanced by the Law, but only tolerated,' et cetera.

The plight of the advocates, who are not recognized by the court, is presented amusingly in physical terms, in the cramped room in which they meet and in the hole in the floor. The onus of the defense is laid on the accused himself, yet the accused has no access to the records; therefore he needs

legal assistance. That is, having no ready access to his unconscious, a patient requires psychiatric help. 'Generally speaking,
an Advocate was not allowed to be present during the examinations, consequently he had to cross-question the accused
immediately after an interrogation, if possible at the very door
of the Court of Inquiry, and piece together from the usually
confused reports he got anything that might be of use for the
Defence.' These examinations are internal to the patient,
consisting of dreams, fantasies, and so on. 'The most important
thing was the Advocate's personal connection with officials of
the Court; in that lay the chief value of the Defence.' This
personal connection, which seems venal when the allegory is
viewed in social terms, is innocent and beneficial in psychoanalysis. It represents the analyst's knowledge of psychic
processes and dynamics, and especially his understanding of
the unconscious and preconscious. Huld mentions the corruption of the 'very lowest grade of the Court organization,' and
the petty advocates, who bribe their way in and sometimes
achieve temporary but 'surprisingly favourable results, on
which the free-lance Advocates prided themselves, spreading
them out as a lure for new clients, but they had no effect on
the further progress of the case, or only a bad effect.' This
refers to 'quacks,' practitioners of hypnotic or faith cures or
other short-cut methods.

'Nothing was of any real value but respectable personal
connections with the highest officials . . .'—i.e. with the unconscious. The court proceedings are usually kept secret from
subordinate officials—a reference to the compartmentizing,
through repression and censorship, of the several mental levels.

. . . it never occurred to the Advocates that they should suggest or insist on any improvements in the system, while—and
this was very characteristic—almost every accused man, even
quite ordinary people among them, discovered from the earliest stages a passion for suggesting reforms which often wasted

time and energy that could have been better employed in other directions. The only sensible thing was to adapt oneself to existing conditions.

This is sound advice from the psychoanalytic point of view. Huld speaks of the 'ever-vengeful officials' and the ruthless nature of the court when challenged—a reference to the effects of damming up psychic energy by repression. 'In many ways the functionaries were like children'—this harping on the infantilism of the unconscious is endless. Huld claims that sometimes a case vanishes 'into remote, inaccessible Courts, where even the accused was beyond the reach of an Advocate.' Kafka may be referring here to a psychosis, which is beyond the reach of psychoanalytic therapy.

Leni.

Leni, Huld's assistant, symbolizes the unconscious, and the erotic element in analysis.

Leni flings a plate against the wall to summon K. She belongs to the unconscious and is a personification of the female libido, of heterosexual object choice, therefore the appeal to the aural sense is proper to her. Leni means light: she is thus presented as a force of good. Characteristically, she bears a candle, which blinds the advocate, who is accustomed to darkness. She symbolizes the erotic as noble. Leni holds Huld's clients by becoming their mistress.

She is described as having a 'doll-like rounded face,' an allusion to infantilism. She does not leave Huld's presence until it is learned that K. and not the uncle has a case to present. As long as Huld thinks that he must deal with Albert he pretends exhaustion and pleads to have Leni with him, as if he were afraid of the domineering Albert, who seems beyond his psychoanalytic province. But when he learns that it is Joseph K. he will deal with, he is suddenly alert. ' "Oh," said the sick man with much more animation, stretching out his hand to K., "forgive me, I didn't notice you. Go now, Leni" . . .' 'It was as if the thought of a sick visit had paralyzed him until now, so rejuvenated did he look as he supported himself on his elbow. . .'

Leni's aggressiveness toward K. is similar to that of the law-court attendant's wife (both are connected with the unconscious) but dissimilar to Fräulein Bürstner's, who represents the real woman in K.'s life. Leni leads K. to the advocate's office. There he sees the portrait of a judge who is, as she explains, only an examining magistrate. The top step leading to the throne-like seat is covered with a yellowish carpet and the seat itself is gilded. Leni offers herself physically but K. is cool. He shows her Elsa's photograph. She says that Elsa is 'very tightly laced.' She refers by innuendo to Elsa's behavior rather than to her clothes. Leni's animal quality is represented by feline features: two of her fingers are connected by a web of skin; K. calls her hand a pretty little paw. She bites his neck, 'biting into the very hairs of his head.' K. is markedly inept and unresponsive under her ministrations.

Titorelli.

Titorelli is the archetype of the anal character. As a painter, he is coprophilic. He is closely connected with the court. As a father imago he offers K. castration threats.

Titorelli's name, a parody on Tintoretto and Botticelli, is revealing. It derives from the German *titte* and *orellin*. *Titte* means teat ('The painter was lolling back in his chair, his nightshirt gaped open, he had thrust one hand inside it and was lightly fingering his breast'). Orellin is, according to Webster, 'a specific name of annatto, alluding to the fact that the Amazon (on the banks of which annatto is common) was discovered by Francisco Orellano.' It is defined as 'a yellow substance obtained from the seeds of annatto.' The reference

[177]

to breast is to infantilism. The reference to yellow is to the anal character.

Titorelli lives in a slum. In describing it Kafka emphasizes openings (♀), noise (the father as aural), the number three (♂), and the color yellow.

In the tenement where the painter lived only one wing of the great double door stood open, and beneath the other wing, in the masonry near the ground, there was a gaping hole out of which, just as K. approached, issued a disgusting yellow fluid, steaming hot, from which a rat fled into the adjoining canal. At the foot of the stairs an infant lay belly down on the ground bawling, but one could scarcely hear its shrieks because of the deafening din that came from a tinsmith's workshop at the other side of the entry. The door of the workshop was open; three apprentices were standing in a half-circle round some object on which they were beating with their hammers. . .

Titorelli is surrounded by debauched and deformed young girls who emphasize the scoptophiliac motif by craning their necks, peering through the keyhole in Titorelli's room, and reporting to each other on the progress within it—'Scarcely had he taken off his jacket when one of the girls cried: "He's taken off his jacket now," and he could hear them all crowding to peer through the cracks and view the spectacle for themselves.' Titorelli significantly wears yellow trousers.

The conception of the unconscious in terms of a vindictive brand of justice, victory, and pursuit, a fitting conception for the castration context, is indicated in the discussions of Titorelli's portrait of the judge. Titorelli describes for K. the three (♂) possibilities of acquittal in his case. Titorelli's anal sadism acts as a castration threat upon K. Titorelli, like K., is fixated (he paints the same picture over and over), stunted (his paintings all show stunted trees), and sadistic. He calls his paintings 'Wild Nature, a heathscape,' probably an allusion to the wildness of the unconscious.

[178]

4. Nomenclature

The nomenclature of *The Trial* is not as allusive as that of *The Castle*, and it does not contain patterns of meaning, as does the later novel. *The Trial* is clearly a more transparent and simple symbolic novel than *The Castle*.

Rabensteiner refers to ravenstone or gallows. Kaminer and Kullich are not quite clear. Kaminer may be derived from the German, *kamin*, chimney, fireplace, Kullich from *kuh*, cow. Kühne (from Deletion 2 of the MS) derives from *kühn* (bold, daring), Wolfart (from Deletion 4 of the MS) from *wolfs-art*, wolfish nature.

Autobiographical references are not lacking. The first, which has been noted by many commentators, is the fact that K.'s age is the same as Kafka's. But a reference that has escaped notice is the use of Kafka's uncles' names. He had four uncles on his mother's side: Albert, Joseph, Rudolf, and Siegfried. Three (♂) of these he selected for the novel, calling K. Joseph, the uncle Albert, and Block Rudi.

An examination of five of *The Trial* fragments is suggestive. The visual factor is strong in 'Journey to his Mother' and altogether transparent in 'The House'—K. gapes at the man dressed like a matador and 'he could not get enough of seeing.' Kafka seems as callous to the figure of the mother as he is to the father, whom he kills off as a very young man. The mother is presented as old, immoderately and unpleasantly pious, and as rather a drudge and burden. Kullich's connection with the court is stated openly in 'Journey to his Mother.' In 'Public Prosecutor' heterosexual object-choice is presented distastefully in the person of Helene (as in Brunelda and the indecent books of the examining magistrate), yet Helene (like Leni) means light, symbolizing the noble. Hasterer may be assumed to stem from the German *hast* (haste or make haste) and to mean one who hastens or makes others hasten. The sexual

symbolism of the wood ($♀$) and the attempt to insert the
pillars ($♂$) of the balustrade into the holes ($♀$) in 'The Fight
with the Deputy Manager' is obvious.

THE MINOR WRITINGS

Amerika. In his first novelistic effort Kafka's allegory
consists largely of father images and the thematic progression
of parts. We have already discussed these. The novel, however,
contains many mythical symbols: three ($♂$) segments, each
composed of three ($♂$) chapters, the sword ($♂$) of the Statue
of Liberty, Karl's box and umbrella, the sea-chest, ship, salami,
money, candles, et cetera. Names are used generally for
onomatopoetic reasons rather than for etymological ones.

The Shorter Fiction. It is not possible, within the scope
of this study, to present a detailed analysis of their symbolism.
A few suggestive notes are appended in the hope that other
investigators will be stimulated to carry the analysis further.

'Investigations of a Dog.' The animal symbolizing passion.
Violent music as coitus. Exhaustion, apprehension, and guilt
caused by coitus. Compulsion to inquiry and investigation a
sublimation of infantile sexuality (cf. Freud's *Leonardo da
Vinci*). Note unusual absence of mythical symbols.

'The Burrow.' The burrow as house, the house as human
form as a whole. The castle keep as woman, mother, womb.
Fear of violence symbolizing fear of coitus. Anal-sadistic,
compulsive tone and matter. Auditory hyperesthesia in the
love of stillness. Anxiety neurosis. Omnipotence of thought in
the virtuoso verbalization of anxiety. Compulsive and cathartic
nature of the writing. Again an absence of mythical symbols.

The Metamorphosis. Vermin symbolizing children. The
bug as Kafka. Paul Goodman, in his recent preface to the
novella, says that Kafka's animals are totems. He neglects to
mention Freud's contribution to the understanding of totem:
the conception of totem as a father symbol. Goodman thinks

[180]

the bug in the novella is a totem. But it symbolizes the son, not the father. In mythical symbolism children are represented by vermin. It is clear that Kafka used the symbol of the bug to represent the son according to Freudian postulates; also because the notion of bug aptly characterized his sense of worthlessness and parasitism before his father. Goodman fails to use the term totem in its original and meaningful context: with the concept of the double taboo against killing the totem and against marrying a person of the same totem clan (parricide and incest).

The Frozen Sea

It is not surprising that the direct influence of Freud on Kafka has gone largely unnoticed and undiscovered, for it has become fashionable, in the last two decades, to underestimate Freud's contribution to our culture while overestimating that of psychoanalysis and of his disciples. Some commentators still claim that Freud is unscientific, apparently overlooking the vast empirical foundation of his work. At present his hidden influence is great, while overt respect for him is slim. This is but one of the aspects of the general current movement toward authoritarianism, witnessed not only in the spreading influence of religions but also in the decline of science in university curricula.

Psychoanalytic studies of Kafka are not rare. Why have they failed to discover the Freudian patterns in the novels? The answer is quite simple. They begin with the assumption that Kafka is not deliberate, and analyze his works as unconscious psychic products, a method that became popular around the middle teens of this century. The method carelessly applies the theories and dynamics of the unconscious to an activity that is largely conscious. In dreams and neurosis the unconscious elements are clear. But in literary composition there is generally no warrant that the work in question was produced in a semi-conscious or altogether unconscious state.

Even in the case of Coleridge's *Kubla Khan,* supposedly composed in a trance, there is room for doubt. To accept unquestioningly an artist's pronouncements about his work is the height of gullibility. The history of literary hoaxes is proof of this—not to speak of an artist's sincere delusions regarding himself. The method is careless also in the aesthetic realm. It makes no distinctions of quality in the objects of its analysis. Everything is grist for its mill—a hack-journalist's column tossed off at the barber's as well as a lyric done with great skill and feeling.

Kafka's novels comprise a fictional equivalent of the infancy period in the human's sexual development, as outlined by psychoanalysis. The three sub-stages of this period, the oral, the anal, and the early genital, are represented by *Amerika, The Trial,* and *The Castle* respectively. The oral *Amerika* portrays Karl's optimism (an oral trait, according to Karl Abraham) and his oral pyrotechnics; *The Trial* Joseph K.'s compulsiveness, sense of guilt, and sadomasochism; *The Castle* K.'s parent object-choice. The anal symbolism in *The Trial* is abandoned for phallic symbolism* in *The Castle.* K. is the only one of the three protagonists who is genital—and he is only partially genital, because of his Oedipus fixation.

It is likely that Kafka's works are more autobiographical than the works of artists whose output is less intense and less cathartic. For daemonic artists like Kafka, art is compulsive, a direct release of inner stresses which threaten to overwhelm them. Assuming that Kafka's inspiration was autobiographical as well as psychoanalytical, one may cautiously observe that he was an obsessional neurotic, an anal type, and that he suffered from a combination of the castration and Oedipus complexes. Details follow in this train of thought: e.g. that Kafka was onanistic, that he broke with F.B. because of his disinclination to coitus, that he suffered from scoptophilia (the visual sense in his diaries is overwhelmingly predominant) and

[183]

auditory hyperesthesia (suggestive are his dislike of music, his sensitivity to noise, as reported by Brod, and his comments on the noisiness of his father in the *Letter*), that he was familiar with an unsuccessful analysis, et cetera.

Kafka writes of psychoanalysis in one of the *Meditations* (undated):

> You say that you do not understand it. Try to understand it by calling it disease. It is one of the many symptoms of disease which psychoanalysis claims to have uncovered. I do not call it disease, and I consider the therapeutic part of psychoanalysis a helpless error. All these so-called diseases, pitiful as they look, are beliefs, the attempts of a human being in distress to cast his anchor in some mother-soil; thus what psychoanalysis finds to be the primary source of religions is none other than the source of individual 'disease.' Today, to be sure, there is no religious unity, the sects are numberless and mostly confined to individuals, or perhaps that is only how it seems to an eye entangled in the present. But such anchorings which find real soil are not a man's individual possession, they are preformed in his being, and afterwards continue to form his being (his body too) further in that direction. Who can hope for cure here?
>
> In my case three circles may be imagined, the innermost one A, then B, then C. The core A explains to B why this man must torment and distrust himself . . . why he may not live. (Was not Diogenes, for instance, gravely ill in that sense? Who among us would not have been overjoyed under the sun-like eye of Alexander? Diogenes, however, desperately begged him to stop obstructing the sunlight. That barrel was full of specters.) C, the man of action, gets no explanation at all, only terrible commands from B; C acts under the strictest pressure, but more in terror than in understanding, he trusts, he believes, that A has explained everything to B and that B has understood everything clearly.

Kafka says that he considers the therapeutic part of psychoanalysis a helpless error. Is he qualified to make such a judgment? One can make the statement intelligently

[184]

as a physician, as a patient, or perhaps as an intimate of a patient. This may be a clue to the fact that Kafka underwent analysis and that it was unsuccessful—perhaps because, like Joseph K., he rejected his 'advocate.'

Extremely interesting is Kafka's use of the three circles to explain himself. Are these not the very same incommensurable mental levels he projected in *The Castle*—the unconscious, preconscious, and conscious of psychoanalysis? How perverse that he should employ the theory of psychoanalysis in an effort to discredit its therapy. The reference to Diogenes and Alexander is also very interesting. Diogenes, Kafka says, was ill when he asked Alexander to stop obstructing the sunlight, because any normal man would have gloried under the sun-like Alexandrian eye. What he means is that he would have gloried under it, under the eye of the father imago, he who wished more than anything else approval from the father. His expression 'sun-like eye' is not as naive as it sounds —Kafka, who knew his symbolism, understood that the word 'sun' transformed Alexander into a father surrogate, since the sun is the greatest father symbol of all. Diogenes, less ill than Kafka, preferred the prime father surrogate, the sun, to a mere human one like Alexander.

Kafka's short and fragmentary autobiographical sketch is an affective verbalization of his castration fears. His suppression as a child, for example in turning off the light to force him to give up reading at night, constitutes a castration threat. What hurt was that his individuality was not being acknowledged. His sense of guilt was progressive. 'It was like receiving a tap with a brush, not intended to hurt, but only as a warning; but one reacted by separating the bristles, drawing their points singly into one's body and beginning to prick and scratch one's inside according to one's own design, while the other's hand is still calmly holding the handle of the brush.'

This fantasy is suggestive: the bristles are penis-like, indicating the author's latent thoughts. Kafka's example of the miser who wishes to make a free confession in order to regain his 'free childhood' (read innocence and mental health) is also suggestive and apt. It involves money, and money is closely connected symbolically with the anal character. The miser's greed, which Kafka so starkly emphasizes, is also related to the anal character. We recall Freud's cardinal triad of anal characteristics: orderliness, parsimony (which may become avarice), and obstinacy (which may become defiance and perhaps irascibility and vindictiveness).

Kafka's proof of genius lies not in the choice of his secret material but in his ability to transmute it into enormously affective dramas and myths. He was not an artistic parasite on the body of psychoanalysis. He explored the relations between neurosis and sociology, myth, religion, literature; and between mental and somatic states, a field that Freud in his later years called the work of the future.

Because of their relation to the father problem, certain literary remarks will not be irrelevant here. Kafka must have been impressed by the contrast between Benjamin Franklin's father and his own; this would account for his interest in the *Autobiography*. When Benjamin wrote his letters to John Collins on 'the propriety of educating the female sex in learning, and their abilities for study,' his father corrected them kindly. Kafka's father in a similar situation would probably have been sarcastic. The influence of the *Autobiography* is very evident in *Amerika*. Young Franklin's wandering from Boston to Philadelphia after running away from home reminds one of Karl Rossmann's wandering in the new land.

Kafka's interest in *David Copperfield* was also probably very personal. David has an ideal father, the one in the graveyard. His step-father, Murdstone, is sadistic. David is

[186]

orphaned, an outcast. His life is a quest for security and belonging. Its similarity to Kafka's and to Karl Rossmann's needs no stressing.

Kafka's interest in Kierkegaard does not necessarily imply an acceptance of the latter's theology. Kierkegaard's similarity to Kafka—in his relations with his father, in his tragic affair with Regina Olsen (which he described secretly and symbolically in *Fear and Trembling*), in his early death—is striking. Undoubtedly Kafka found consolation in studying his life, especially at a time when he was suffering in his relations with his father and with F.B. As for the Abraham story, of which Kierkegaard made so much, and which the cabalists claim to be incorporated in the Amalia episode of *The Castle*, Kierkegaard withheld half of the drama. His emphasis on Abraham can be rebutted by an emphasis on Isaac. If Abraham's relation is with God, Isaac's is with Abraham. From Isaac's point of view, Abraham's faith is a crime against him. It is precisely this, the relation of the son to the father who has frightened him with the sacrificial knife, that was both Kierkegaard's and Kafka's problem, the problem of the castration complex. This context explains their interest in the fable. But Kierkegaard lived in the age of the dominance of the father, Kafka in the age of the revolt of the son. That is why Kierkegaard emphasized Abraham's role and eventually returned to the father by way of the church, and why Kafka emphasized Isaac's role and destroyed himself in a progressive revolt.

The parallel between Kafka and D. H. Lawrence is suggestive. They were born two years apart and died six years apart. Both were neurotic, both Oedipus types, both tubercular. Both dealt with sexual themes—Kafka secretly, Lawrence openly, Kafka in a cool symbolic prose, Lawrence in a prose dithyrambic and a little sticky.

Young writers, seeking new things to say and new ways of saying them, and caught in a transitional, chaotic period in which artistic as well as political and ethical values are uncertain, are often depressed by the spectacle of literary dead-ends. The recognized masters are not easily to be followed, if at all. The density and sublety of James are overwhelming and, although easy to parody, difficult to imitate creatively. Joyce's explorations of consciousness, language, and myth stand like vaguely threatening Egyptian pyramids, depressing to those who, with the hope of continuing where he left off, contemplate the skill, energy, and erudition which account for them. Mann's exquisite orchestral renderings of symbol, myth, disease, and idea seem the last word in a sort of underwater endurance. And the sensibility and mass, the incredible detail and paralyzing architecture of Proust, are almost beyond even parody. The age of the literary titans in the field of the novel seems to be drawing to a close and the young writer wonders where, creatively speaking, he is to go. A few writers still blindly follow the fortunes of naturalism, although that school was considered played out more than half a century ago. Some play with a Lawrencian lyricism, although Lawrence languishes as a potent force. Some are tentatively trying myth or toying with existentialism. Others carry on the muckraker tradition, both in the romantic and realistic veins. The southern school of the *outré* still staggers on. The American and earlier, unsystematic version of *ça existe*, most successfully exploited by Hemingway, is pretty much done for. Music, symbol, dream, revolution, idea, myth—what is the young writer to do with them and how is he to handle them fruitfully and originally?

In their despair some writers have gone to Kafka and the surrealists, confusing the two, adopting the appearance of Kafka as the reality and proceeding with psychological experiments that are essentially sterile. But Kafka's imitators have failed because they have not grasped his essential meaning and have therefore misinterpreted his use of forms and symbols; besides, they have been insufficiently aware of the autobiographical content and inspiration of his work. Kafka seems, at first hand, to be the only important modern novelist not strongly dependent on autobiography, and this is somehow attractive and seductive, probably because too many critics have complained of the monotony of autobiographical novels of a sensitive childhood, tormented adolescence, and neurotic and rebellious adulthood. But Kafka, in the great modern tradition, is highly autobiographical. Therein lies his power, validity, and significance. This is one of the chief lessons to be learned from him by those who would follow on the tight-rope of greatness. Kafka is attractive for other reasons. He provides an example of complexity and profundity without bewildering erudition, massive canvas, or exhausting verbal innovation. He indicates the value, the freshness of the irrational rationally applied, shows how to present the psychologically abnormal from within. There is also the fact of Kafka's timeliness, which we have already mentioned. His world, like ours, is oppressed, distraught, and barely intelligible.

Having just emphasized Kafka's strong points, which I have been asserting throughout this study, perhaps this is the place to speak of his limitations. What has most disconcerted me at times is Kafka's thematic monotony as well as the closeness of his world. His world is airless and I have often desired to refresh myself by a perusal of a world more approximate to the real—particularly the world of Tolstoy, with its emphasis on action and natural scenery. One tires of hospitals and sanitaria, much as one sympathizes with their inmates. There is also the item of canvas—Kafka really accomplished little in this respect, compared with his Olympian contemporaries. And his works are mainly unfinished, to his detriment. Unfortunately he died young, but Tolstoy, had he died at the same age, would have written *War and Peace*.

Kafka, like the Symbolists, preferred suggestion to explicit statement, but unlike them he did not deliberately employ the devices of music as a technique. He used the irrational and infantile—and the special brand of symbolism of the unconscious psyche—to achieve his anti-cerebral effects. There is the fluidity of music, a fragility, in the work of the Symbolists which is absent in Kafka's lithographic surface, yet the repetition of certain motifs and symbols in Kafka has a mathematically musical effect antithetical to the Wagnerian mysticism and sensuousness of the Symbolists. The Symbolists, as is well known, no more invented symbolism than Dante did; they simply employed personal symbolism, i.e. symbolism chosen or created by a purely personal association of ideas, to an extreme extent. They popularized the personal or subjective symbol at the expense of the social or objective one, such as fish, lamb (symbols of Christ), ship (early symbol of the church), peacock (immortality), flag, cross, et cetera. In doing so they reasserted the value of the subject as against the object at a time when literary naturalism seemed to have come to a dead end with its exorbitant interest in the object. Since the Symbolists were pre-Freudian they could not use mythical symbols knowingly; such symbols in their work resulted from the natural proportion of unconscious elements in their creative activity, derived from a knowledge of dreams, myths, folklore, neurosis, and the usual wellings up of the unconscious mind during the creative act. Kafka exploited mythical symbolism as deliberately as the Symbolists exploited personal symbolism. In doing so he went further than two other similar literary pioneers, Mann and Joyce, for he created whole patterns out of this type of symbol. He did not neglect the social or personal factors but carefully selected social symbols, such as castle, which also possess a mythical value, and often fused into these a highly personal element.

If one is inclined, as some observers are, to regard the distinction of the modern outlook as intimately related to the discovery of the importance of symbolization (the two chief forms under current scrutiny of which are psychological symbolism and symbolic logic), one may easily regard Kafka as the first great modern symbolist, for whom the Symbolists were suggestive forerunners. His symbolic world, with its candles, photographs, abasia, coughing, invalidism, insects, animals, numbers, fragments of autobiography, special colors, and what-not, is indubitably modern, dating the symbolism that preceded it. Like the Symbolists, Kafka is essentially romantic, anti-naturalistic (in the literary sense). Like such romantics as Byron, Chateaubriand, Mallarmé, Verhaeren, Claudel, Huysmans, and Verlaine, and unlike such classicists as Racine, Molière, Dryden, and Swift, he is interested primarily in the subject, not the object. But unlike the Symbolists, he is interested in the subject *as* object: he applies the rigorous method of realism to levels subsisting beneath the conscious mind. In a sense he fuses realism and symbolism, classicism and romanticism. Thomas Mann, a great favorite of Kafka's, achieves a similar result by somewhat different means. As long ago as *Royal Highness* (1909) he was 'feeling after new things.' He himself has written of that novel: 'For this as I saw it was my problem as an artist: how to take the serious and weighty naturalism I had inherited from the nineteenth century and faithfully practised, and loosen and lighten, heighten and brighten it into a work of art which should be intellectual and symbolical, a transparency for ideas to shine through.' What Mann achieved in terms of the conscious Kafka achieved on sub-conscious levels. Mann, despite his preoccupation with disease, is a child of light compared to Kafka. Kafka's brand of romanticism implies an insistence on the importance of the unconscious beyond anything dreamed even by Schopenhauer; unlike the early romantics he underlines the importance of the element Jung calls the collective and Freud the phylogenetic unconscious. Kafka's drama is the striving of the egoistic and social to merge. He does not hold the mirror up to nature in the sense of nature as object; he holds it up before himself, the modern mind. Realism, impressionism, and naturalism imitate the object. Kafka rejects these (except as devices) in favor of expressionism, the art of the subject, of myth, dream, ritual, language—and neurosis.

The discovery of the importance of symbolization has paralleled the decline of the conception of language as a purely utilitarian, communicational system of symbols. Studies of the irrational and primitive, of ritual, magic, and folklore have provided key insights into the pervasive function of expression. Symbolism and expressionism are closely related, both entailing expressivity, the externalization of the subject, of psychic energy. In the case of Kafka it is seen how the two processes intermingle and strengthen each other. A number of critics have denied that Kafka is an expressionist, mainly because he was not an active member of the German expressionist movement. They have confused the provincial term as applied to that movement with the more universal term too seldom used to denote the whole modern movement.

It seems clear that the modern 'isms' have in common the elements of distortion, dissonance, and irrationality and that they can be fruitfully considered as part of a broad movement, known as expressionism, which is romantic, revolutionary and anti-cerebral. A few improvised definitions may be helpful, for all their crudity, in distinguishing the expressionist movement from its predecessors. If realism is the selection of data with intent to interpret and imitate the object, and if impressionism is the selection of data with intent to interpret and imitate the object in such a manner as to comment on the subject, and if naturalism is the selection of data with intent to interpret and to imitate the object in such a manner as to comment on the object, then expressionism is the selection of data with intent to interpret and to imitate the subject in such a manner as to comment on the object. In expressionism the result is distortion only because the subject, especially that part of it which is unconscious, distorts the object; where the intention is to distort rather than to imitate, the result is sensationalism and pseudo-expressionism. Much of the confusion concerning Kafka's expressionist position centers around his use of a classic prose style (his bond with tradition and his refusal to indulge in sensationalism) and a confusion of his brand of expressionism with the pseudo-expressionism of many lesser writers contemporaneous with him.

Benedetto Croce lists expressionism, in the *Encyclopædia Britannica*, as among the romantic movements which hate museums as repositories of the 'old' art. In the first place, he uses the term in a narrow sense and in the second, he ascribes a violence of revolt to the romantic movement in general which is unjustified by the examination of certain examples such as Kafka. Nevertheless the element of revolt *is* strong in expressionism and in Kafka although its chief object is not the 'old' art but the authority of the father, however it masquerades itself. No doubt the modern artist is justified in his revolt after a century in which the father's rule was tyrannical. By the turn of the century the pride of the father was ripe for a fall. His powerful position had been undermined by scientific attacks against the church, which considered children to be soaked in original sin that had to be sternly repressed; and by the dawning insights into father-son relationships publicized by the psychoanalytic movement; as well as by the onslaughts against the remnants of pre-scientific secular authority (in some parts of Europe still in the form of feudalism) occasioned by technological and ethical advances. The litera-

[193]

ture of revolt against the father was already considerable before the advent of expressionism. Expressionism raised to a howl what had only been a sullen murmur. But antagonistic toward the father though he was, Kafka mingled with his revolt an understanding of and respect for the vital elements of tradition.

A note on Kafka's humor. His laughter is never loud; it is cloudy and inhibited, for it is never far removed from its object. His is an Eastern, a Slavic strain of humor, the humor of the underdog, of the Czech, the Jew, the Russian peasant broken by poverty. One thinks of Sholem Aleichem, Ivan Olbracht, Jaroslav Hašek, and some of the peasant stories of F. C. Weiskopf; one thinks of Gorki, Chekhov, Joseph Wittlin's *Salt of the Earth*. Kafka's humor is the humor of pain, with empathy for the tragic object. Solid laughter is divorced from its object, it has perspective on it; Kafka's laughter is ambivalent, it is close to tears. Its wincing quality is its moral tone; in Kafka the 'web of maya' flutters in shreds. In reading Gogol one laughs aloud, the humor is riotous, verging on the burlesque; involved in a comedy of manners, it contains its share of sadness, so that Pushkin is said to have remarked of a portion of *Dead Souls*, 'Oh, God, how sad our Russia is!' But it is uninhibited. One rarely laughs aloud when reading Kafka; loud laughter in him would seem a sign of callousness; one winces while smiling inwardly. Humor is an element of suspense in Kafka; its cathartic effect is slight. Kafka is almost never witty. He does not say, in the way of Molière, 'He makes his cook his merit, and the world visits his dinners and not him.' His is the humor of dreams, madness, the irrational, the clandestine slyly revealed; it is rarely intellectual or icily mordant like Swift's. It is the comedy of the fly writhing on the fly-paper, horrible, a little sardonic, yet with the awful morality of one who prefers death to the common delusions that make life bearable. It is the humor of night-dreams, dreams that mock our day-lives.

The comic, said Bergson, 'is something mechanical encrusted upon the living,' an observation often realized in Kafka by means of his satire on bureaucracy. Bureaucracy in Kafka is like the machine in a Chaplin film, which has got out of hand and goes human; Kafka's robots recall the scene in *Modern Times* in which Chaplin, having left the assembly line, still goes through the involuntary motions of tightening bolts, unable to quiet the mechanical in him. Kafka is full of the infantile, incongruous and exaggerated. In his novels adults are children playing at reason and maturity, at cross-purposes with themselves. Kafka is expert in exploding the pretensions of the conscious mind by suddenly revealing the power of the unconscious. Kafka's humor is that of the awful, of disease. Together with his sense of tragedy it reveals man as neither the godlike child of reason of the classical age nor the Olympian, pantheistic savage of the romantic age, but rather the fumbling, half-baked hybrid stuck fast mid-way between the animal and the spiritual. Kafka fictionally echoed Blaise Pascal, who once wrote: 'What a chimera, then, is man! What a novelty, what a monster, what a chaos, what a subject of contradiction, what a prodigy! A judge of all things, feeble worm of the earth, depository of the truth, cloaca of uncertainty and error, the glory and the shame of the universe!'